Developing Strong Black Male Ministries

By Jawanza Kunjufu

Chicago, Illinois

First Edition, First Printing

Front cover illustration by Harold Carr

Text illustrations by Angelo Williams

Copyright © 2006 by Dr. Jawanza Kunjufu

All rights reserved.

Printed in the United States of America

ISBN #: 0974900095

CONTENTS

INTRODUCTION

Is your church attractive to the following men?
- illiterate
- high school dropouts
- unemployed
- underemployed
- working poor
- homeless
- gang member
- felon
- angry
- aggressive
- high-energy
- short attention span

In 1994, I wrote the bestseller *Adam, Where Are You? Why Most Black Men Don't Go to Church.* I was concerned then, and now, about the dangerously low numbers of men that attend church. On average, 25 to 40 percent of church congregations in America are male. When you analyze male attendance by age group and race, as I do in this book, *Developing Strong Black Male Ministries,* the picture is even more disturbing.

In addition to my consulting work with school districts, I am often asked to preach at churches. Over the years, I have had the honor of preaching at hundreds of churches and church-sponsored events and to thousands of pastors, church leaders, and parishioners about the population that I've been called, by God, to work with, minister to, and advocate for: African American males in the following categories—boys, adolescents, teenagers, young adults, adults, and mature adults.

From my work in schools, I have come to the inescapable conclusion that the only way the many problems facing African American males will be resolved is through the church. Only our Lord and Savior Jesus Christ has the answer to our problems and the power to heal and prosper us. Only through Jesus will the Black man rise to take his rightful place as head and priest in the family and leader in the community. So my perspective, strategies, and paradigm are unapologetically Christian (first) and African-centered.

Whenever I am given the pulpit in a church, one of the first things I will do is ask the men in the congregation to stand. Whether I am preaching in a small church or large, it is awesome to see Black men of all hues, shapes, sizes, and ages stand up. At some mega-churches I have had more than a thousand men stand up, and this inspires me. When men stand up together there is a sense of strength, unity, and purpose that all in the Lord's house can feel.

And then I have the women stand. Whether in a small church or large, the story is the same. Two to three times more women than men will stand up. There are so many women, and so few men by comparison, that you have to remind yourself that the men are there, because when all those women stand, it almost makes the men disappear.

Whether the church has 300 members with 100 males or 3,000 members with 1,000 males, we are still looking for Adam. In the Adam Update chapter, we will look at 21 reasons that explain why Adam is absent from the church. These reasons peer deeply into man's nature, and they will help us design ministries to effectively meet his spiritual (first), physical, psychological, social, and financial needs.

I am concerned not only about Adam Sr. but Adam Jr. Isn't it interesting that the group causing the greatest havoc in the Black community—12 to 19-year-old males—is least represented in church congregations? As we will examine in the Teenage Male Ministries chapter, as the church develops strong ministries designed specifically for young Black males, we will begin to see drastic reductions, even eliminations, of the problems facing our community as a whole.

In my book *Hip Hop Street Curriculum*, I describe the impact that rap is having on our youth. I also try to understand our youth, what they value and why they are so mesmerized with rappers like 50 Cent. We should all be concerned that 50 Cent and others like him are having a greater impact on teenage males than our Lord and Savior, Jesus Christ.

There is a reason why rappers are more attractive to youth than Jesus. Since the European Middle Ages, Jesus has been portrayed as White, blonde, blue-eyed, and wimpish. As a result, Black males have chosen the hard-core image of gangster rappers over the White, blue-eyed Jesus of European fantasy. In the Masculine Jesus chapter, we will look at this dichotomy. Based on my study of scripture, I will present a more truthful image of Jesus, a strong man, a fearless leader and revolutionary, that will help Black males put gangster rappers in their proper perspective. Our youth need to see the real Jesus, His masculinity and strength.

At the many Men's Days, conferences, and events where I have had the honor of preaching, the themes have been dramatic and reflect the urgency of the church to reach out and minister to Black males. Some of the conference themes have included titles such as, "Where Is the Black Man?" "Adam, Where Are You?" and "How to Empower the Black Man." Because the needs of Black males are so great, the topics seem endless.

Despite the many worthy attempts of churches nation-wide to minister to Black males, I wonder if our approach has kept pace with the demands of the times. Are we being too religious and traditional in our programs and conferences, our Sunday morning services? Despite all the excitement generated by publicity and planning, do the actual events ultimately stand up to and meet the needs of men? Are we still thinking and planning in the box of religion and tradition? Do men leave these events any better than the way they entered? Are these events truly life changing? Do they empower Black men, strengthen Black men, and bring Black men to Christ?

After the men have gone home, are we evaluating the effectiveness of our events? Beyond the number of men who responded to the altar call or the offerings that were collected, have men's lives been changed for the better? How do we measure and track progress? How do we conduct follow-up with attendees?

Remember the story of David and Goliath? When David's elder brother chastises him for leaving his sheep in the wilderness to watch the battle unfold, David raises a prophetic question in 1 Samuel 17:29: "Is there not a cause?"

This book and all my books have been written because I have a cause. In 1980, 100,000 African American males were incarcerated and/or involved with the penal system (e.g., probation). In 2006, one of every three African American males is involved in the penal system, i.e., more than 1.5 million. Is there not a cause?

Satan is projecting that by 2020, two of every three African American males will be involved in the penal system. Is there not a cause?

In the Teenage Male Ministries chapter, I describe a violent confrontation between a funeral service in a church and a gang. Is there not a cause?

When you have a church filled with elders and women but very few men, and in some churches no African American males between 12 and 19 years of age, is there not a cause?

When families, schools, and churches are dominated and populated by Black women and young men can barely be found, is there not a cause?

Developing Strong Black Male Ministries will look at these issues, these causes, and then, of course, we will look at how the church can truly empower Black men individually and as a group.

We cannot develop strong ministries until we develop strong men. Because men are not a homogeneous group, I have found it helpful to break down the discussion by age group. Each age group has its own unique set of needs. In the last few chapters on developing strong, effective ministries for men, we will review typical ministries and the roles that Black men play, and we will look at ministries specifically designed for teenagers (12 to 19 years), young adults (20 to 35 years), and mature men (35 years and over). In particular, I am concerned about Black males 12 to 35 years of age because of their under representation in the church. Despite their great personal and social needs, they are virtually invisible in the church. Clearly the church has not made a good case for men's ministry. Teen and young adult males look for other ways, not always positive, to meet their needs. Hopefully, with this book and others, this will begin to change.

We need churches that will do more than provide men's fellowship primarily run by elderly men who may be out of touch with the needs of younger men. It's a new day, and the strategies that worked in the past are no longer effective. To compete against gangster rappers and gangs, the strategies I present in the Prison/Drugs/Street/AIDs Ministries chapter can become an essential cornerstone of an effective church. The anointed church would never allow liquor stores and crack houses as their neighbors, and we will see how churches have actually dealt with these problems.

The chapter Mature Adult Ministries looks at developing strong elder ministries with an emphasis on health and the impact that prostate cancer has had on Black men. African American males lead the world in prostate cancer, and this is unacceptable. We will also look at many other needs this group faces on a daily basis, including financial/retirement and psychological well being.

I thought long and hard about the final chapter on homosexuality and its impact on the church, particularly on heterosexual male attendance. It would be politically expedient and correct for me to avoid this issue, just as politicians avoid certain topics because of the potential loss of votes or funds. It reminds me of the minister who runs for office on the platform that as a minister, he is against homosexuality and abortion but as a politician he is in full support. Pastors who are afraid to preach what the Bible says about homosexuality because of the potential negative impact on their budget and choir membership are attempting to serve two masters.

In the spirit of Matthew 6:24, I serve only one master: "No man can serve two masters; for either he will hate the one and love the other, or else he will hold to the one and despise the other. Ye cannot serve God and mammon."

I am a writer, not a politician. I'm not trying to be politically correct. I'm trying to be biblically correct. Adam Sr. and Adam Jr. are not in the church because they see that the church is filled with women, elders, and "sissies." They see images of Jesus as wimpish and White. Much more will be said about this issue in later chapters.

Thank you for reading this book. I pray that the insights into men's needs and the strategies for developing strong Black male ministries presented throughout will support your church's efforts to meet the needs of men. I hope you will share it with your friends. I pray it will make a difference in your life.

In the next chapter, we will look at some thought-provoking anecdotes.

CHAPTER 1:
THOUGHTS, INSIGHTS, AND ANECDOTES

✝ The greatest legacy a father can
ever give to his child
is faith.

✝ When you save a man,
you save a family.

✝ When a child accepts Jesus
as Lord, 4 percent of
the family will follow.
When a mother accepts Jesus
as Lord, 17 percent of the
family will follow.
When a father accepts Jesus as
Lord, 93 percent of the
family will follow.

✝ You cannot have effective male ministries until you have effective men.

✝ Jesus did not say, "Go and make workers." He said, "Go and make them disciples" (Matthew 28:19). Too often we try to make workers and pray for disciples. Have we placed service over worship?

✝ The greatest tragedy to the American family was the Industrial Revolution. Before then, fathers and sons worked together on the farm.

✝ Time equals influence. As a result, peers, rappers, and television are raising our children.

✝ A female dominated Sunday School will lead to a female dominated church.

✝ Does 50 Cent have a greater influence on Black male youth than Jesus Christ?

✝ Most men have attended church at least once. Men don't go to church because they've already been and there was something missing.

✝ Even a church full of beautiful Black women is not enough to attract and keep a man in church.

✝ More than 90 percent of Jesus' ministry was done **outside** the church. If the church does not go into the streets to recapture an entire generation of young, poor, Black males, the streets will violently come inside the church.

✝ Men are changed by what they experience, not by what they are told. Sermons do not change behavior.

✝ Satan is not afraid of a sermon.
Satan is afraid of the **Word.**

✝ Most worshippers pimp the
preacher and rely solely on
the sermon to take them
through the week.

✝ There is a difference between a
male, a boy, and a man.
A person is born male.
He grows into a boy, and
boys like to play.
Young boys play with cars
and trucks.
Old boys play with women
and their children.
Men are responsible.
They work before they play.

✝ An affair is an escape from
reality. One of the best
ways to avoid an affair is
to pray for your wife daily.

✝ There is a difference between
hot forbidden sex in dating
or an affair and
emotionally connected
married sex.

✝ Should we design the worship
service for the 65-year-old
female or for the 16-year-old
male?

✝ When Jesus rose, that was the Resurrection. When Jesus called Lazareth out after four days, that was a resurrection. Every time a Black man stands up for Jesus and puts down drugs and his negative lifestyle, that is a resurrection.

✝ Just because a wife earns more income than her husband, that does not make her head of the house.

✝ The Black family cannot survive with Jezebel in charge and Ahab allowing it.

CHAPTER 2:
BIBLICAL TRUTHS

Biblical Truth 1. You are a saint, not a sinner saved by grace.

A sinner saved by grace is an oxymoron. You are either a sinner or you were saved by grace. If you have been saved by grace, you are no longer a sinner.

In almost every letter Paul wrote in the New Testament, he refers to his Christian brethren as saints. Nowhere in the Bible do you read the phrase, "a sinner saved by grace." Now this does not mean that a saint does not sin, but Christ's sacrifice on the Cross remits us from sin (i.e., blots it out).

There is an interesting distinction between a sin and a saint: one is a noun and one is a verb. The noun (saint) determines our identity, while the verb (sin) describes our behavior in a situation. When I do parent workshops, I always recommend to parents that they criticize the child's behavior but never attack the child and his character. This is the same idea.

When Christians apply the term "sinner" to themselves rather than their behavior, this gives them *carte blanche* sin privileges. "Well you know, I'm just a sinner saved by grace." "I couldn't help myself, because that's what sinners do." "I'm only human." "The devil made me do it." Our Lord and Savior does not see us as sinners. He sees us as saints.

Just as it is has been important for us to evolve from seeing ourselves as Negro or colored to Africans, African Americans, or Africans in America, it is even more important in the sight of God to know that we have rights, that we can come boldly to the throne of grace, not as a sinner but as a saint.

Biblical Truth 2. The Lord gives and the Lord does *not* take away.

Job says in Job 1:21, "The Lord gave and the Lord has taken away." Since then, some preachers have used this scripture to try and explain suffering. How many times have I heard a preacher say during the funeral service, "The Lord gave and the Lord has taken away." I heard this scripture at the homegoing services of a baby and a teenage male, the victim of a drive-by shooting. I heard it at the service of young Black mother, an active member of her church, who died from cancer. Memorial services remembering the victims of 9/11 and hurricane Katrina were eulogized with, "The Lord gave and the Lord has taken away."

One of the reasons why Adam Sr. and Adam Jr., and even Eve Sr. and Eve Jr. are not involved in church is because many of them are mad at God because the pastor said that the Lord took their loved one. The Lord caused 9/11 and Katrina. They believe that God killed those victims.

Along these same lines, I have heard people make asinine statements like, "The Lord put this sickness on me because He wanted to get my attention" or "He wanted to teach me something" or "He's punishing me." If you follow that train of thought, which has no logic in it, this means we have been praying to God for healing, the same God who is making us sick. Does this make sense to you?

Ignorance and long-term suffering have caused us to misinterpret the scriptures. This coming Sunday morning, a Black preacher somewhere in America will preach the story of Job and end with the punchline, "The Lord gave and the Lord has taken away." But the story of Job continues to a positive conclusion, thanks to God's favor and grace on Job's life. It is a misrepresentation to end a sermon with "The Lord gave and the Lord has taken away." Why would God be so capricious to give, then take away, and then give again? It doesn't make sense, does it?

10

Biblical Truths

In John 10:10, Jesus says, "The thief does not come except to steal, and to kill, and to destroy." And then He says, to make it perfectly clear, "I have come that they may have life, and that they may have it more abundantly." Satan stole Job's wealth, killed his family, and destroyed his life. God had nothing to do with the evil that occurred to Job, but God had everything to do with Job's restoration.

The same is true of your life. When sickness, disease, financial losses, divorce, and death occur, that's the work of Satan. That's an attack of the devil.

This is why it is so important to know your daddy's voice. We must become prayer warriors, doing spiritual battle against the enemy, so that he will keep his dirty paws off our lives and the lives of our loved ones. The still, small voice of the Holy Spirit will guide you through the toughest trials and persecutions. He will move you out of harm's way. Does that sound like "The Lord gave and the Lord has taken away"?

A friend volunteered for a concert fundraiser recently held at a top hotel in Chicago. From the first moment her assignment began, her behavior was strange, even to her. For example, even though sandwiches were offered free of charge, she refused the food—"And I seldom refuse free food," she said. Later, after her duties were completed, for some reason, she didn't know why, she quickly rushed to coat check, grabbed her coat, and fled the hotel like something was chasing her. During the drive home, she wondered why she had behaved this way. Why had she left before the concert had even begun?

The next day, the local newspaper reported that more than 100 people at the same event she attended had gotten sick, and some had to be hospitalized. She had been led and protected before, so in hindsight, she recognized the workings of the Holy Spirit and her angels. My friend said that she didn't hear God's voice so much as she felt compelled, almost pushed out the hotel door. We each hear God's voice in different ways.

Before my biological father passed, I knew his voice. Not just the tone or quality of his voice, but I could predict what he would say.

My name *Jawanza* means "dependable." I got it legally from my father, who was the most dependable person I've ever met. If my father said he would call me every night at 8:00 from work, I could take that promise to the bank. If my father said he was going to combine his lunch and breaks to attend my track meet, debate tournament, or choir concert, I could always count on him being in the stands, supporting me and my classmates every step of the way.

That's what happens when you know your daddy's voice. It is obvious that many of us do not know our Father's voice. If we did, we would know that God did not say, "The Lord gave and the Lord has taken away." That was Job talking out of his anguish and fear. In the 42 chapters of that book, he went through many such turbulent emotions.

God had nothing to do with the infant dying in her crib, the teen victim of the drive-by shooting, the mother who died of cancer, 9/11, or hurricane Katrina. If you want to know your Father, read John 10:10: "Satan comes to kill, to steal, and to destroy."

Yes, it was Satan. Satan masterminded the deaths of the infant, teenager, mother, 9/11, and Katrina. God came to give you life and to give you life more abundantly. There are too many people that are mad at God, and many of them are mad at God because of what was said in the pulpit.

Biblical Truth 3. Malachi 3:8: Man robs God when he does not tithe.

Malachi 3:8 ("Will a man rob God?") refers to the tithe, the 10 percent of our income we give to God. Even though the church needs money to operate, Christians apparently do not feel responsible for tithing, even to support their own church. I have heard that, on the low side, only 4 percent of Christians are tithers. On the high side, maybe 26 percent, which is also unacceptable. Malachi 3:9 says, "You are cursed with a curse."

There is a reason why so many families have seen generations of divorce, drug addiction, alcoholism, pornography, poverty, depression, and suicide. Americans spend 23 percent of their money on debt. Can you imagine that? We're not talking about receiving anything of value for this payment. We're just talking about the interest on the mortgage, the car, the credit cards, and loans.

When preaching in churches, I often ask members who are debt free to stand up. And I thought our greatest problem was the shortage of Black men in church! In some churches, not one adult can stand up and say he is debt free. Yet, clearly, God wants us to prosper. John 3:2 reads, "Beloved, I pray that you prosper in all things and be in health just as your soul prospers." Those who are in debt are enslaved to the world's economic system. Debt is not God's plan for your finances. Prosperity cannot flow to us when we are in debt.

Often, when ministers speak about tithing, they get labeled "prosperity preachers" who preach a "prosperity gospel." I do not like labels. People like to label others to control them. You're a democrat, republican, conservative, liberal, Africentric, or a nationalist. The label "prosperity gospel" implies that the gospel being preached is not full or complete, that it's only a part of scripture. Interestingly, many traditional churches that refuse to address the economic needs of their members and the community are the first to use this label. I contend that if you do not preach the prosperity of Jesus that you're not preaching the full gospel, the whole truth. Didn't Jesus just say in John 3:2, "Beloved, I pray that you prosper in all things and be in health just as your soul prospers"? It's amazing how a church will claim to be Bible believing but then selectively exclude the parts of the Bible they don't agree with:

"We are a Bible believing church, but we don't believe in speaking in tongues."

"We are a Bible believing church, but we endorse homosexuality."

"We are a Bible believing church, but we don't believe in laying hands on the sick."

"We are a Bible believing church, but we don't believe in prosperity."

What I love most about John 3:2 is the balance, like Ma'at, in the scripture. "Beloved, I pray that you prosper in all things and be in health just as your soul prospers." It reminds me of Matthew 6:33: "Seek ye first the Kingdom of God and his righteousness and all these things will follow." The scripture is clear that money should not be more important than your soul. Money should not be more important than your relationship with the Lord.

One of the best ways to show that you love Him is to walk forth on faith and believe that it would be better to live off of 90 percent and give your Lord and Savior 10 than to naively think that you could do a better job living off of 100 percent.

It takes faith to tithe. It requires a personal relationship with the Lord to tithe. And that's why, at best, 26 percent of Christians are tithers. John 3:2 describes prosperity as far more than money. It's a relationship with Him, it's being in health, it's living and being loved by your family.

Ironically, some of the same naysayers of the prosperity message spend an enormous amount of time thinking about their debt. It is difficult to fulfill Jesus' commands to feed the hungry, clothe the naked, preach and take His gospel to the world without money.

Biblical Truth 4. Proverbs 18:21: "Death and life are in the power of the tongue."

In Hebrews 11 and Genesis 1, God framed His world by His words. It is very important to watch what you say. When you are being arrested, the police officer reminds you that you have the right to remain silent. Anything you say can and will be held against you.

Biblical Truths

In the scriptures, Jesus teaches us that it is best to pray the Word. Too many times in churches at altar call and at prayer time, people will get on their knees and pray and thank God for their healing, then they will get up and leave the church and complain to their friends about their sickness. Which statement did you believe? Do you believe "By his stripes you are healed" (Isaiah 53:5)? Or do you believe that your feet are killing you?

If God framed the world by His Words, the least we can do is frame our day by His Word. This is the day the Lord has made. I choose to rejoice and be glad in it (Psalm 118:24).

If you wake up depressed and allow life's challenges to convince you that today is going to be a terrible day, so it will be. You must frame your world by your words. The Bible teaches us that "as a man thinks in his heart, so is he" (Proverbs 23:7). If women say "I'm never going to find a man," they won't. If you say, "I'm always going to be broke," you will.

It can be difficult to "call those things that be not as though they were" (Romans 4:17)—when you are broke, sick, and without a mate. That's why the Bible teaches that the natural man cannot discern spiritual things. If you do not have faith, it will be virtually impossible to say you are healed when you feel sick in your body. If you do not have faith, you cannot claim a mate when there appears to be no good men or women around. If you do not have faith, you cannot claim financial prosperity.

In Mark 9:23, Jesus says, "If you can believe, all things are possible to him who believes." We have to walk by faith and not by sight.

In Mark 11:23–24, Jesus says,

"Assuredly I say to you, whomever *says* to this mountain, be removed and be cast into the sea and does not doubt in his heart but believes that those things he *says* will be done, he will have whatever he *says*. Therefore I say to you, whatever things you ask when you *pray* believe that you receive them and you will have them" (emphasis mine).

15

Note the ratio between say and pray. There's a three to one ratio in this scripture. You do not get what you pray for. You get what you **say**.

This may be controversial, but you do not get what you prayed for in church. You get what you **say** because you believe what you say. It is obvious that what you prayed for in church is not what you believe because if you believed it you could say the wildest, boldest, most outrageous statements in the name of Jesus to your friend on the telephone and not care if he thought you were crazy. If you truly believed, you could say things like:

"The doctor's report was evil. God says I'm healed, and so I'm healed."

"I'm a multimillionaire."

"You may think there are no good women, but I am surrounded by good women, and one of them is already my wife!"

"I'm buying that house on the hill debt-free."

It takes faith to say "I'm healed" when the X-rays or blood tests say otherwise. Just as Jesus spoke to fig trees, we can speak to mountains, and with faith, *they will move.*

Biblical Truth 5. You are in a war between your flesh and your spirit.

Romans 7:8: "But sin, taking opportunity by the commandment, produced in me all manner of evil desire. For apart from the law sin was dead."

Romans 7:21–24 reads,

"I find then a law, that evil is present with me, the one who wills to do good. For I delight in the law of God according to the inward man. But I see another law in my members, warring against the law of my mind, and bringing me into captivity to the law of sin which is in my members. O wretched man that I am!"

Biblical Truths

You are in a war between your flesh and your spirit. Have you ever heard a minister say, "I looked at my hands and they looked new? I looked at my feet and they did too." That reminds me of a sinner saved by grace. Where is that in the Bible? Nowhere in the Bible does it say, "I looked at my hands and they looked new. I looked at my feet and they did too." I hate to burst your bubble, but when you got saved, your flesh did not get saved. Your breath still smells before you brush your teeth. You still have toe jams. You still need to shower. The flesh is never satisfied. It wants all the sex, all the crack, all the liquor, all the ice cream, all the meat, all the cheese, all the pizza—you fill in the blank. The flesh is never satisfied.

You are in a war, and you cannot win a war if you don't first recognize that you are in it. You need to know your enemy. You need to know what's involved in this war. When you got saved, your spirit got saved, but not your flesh.

Visualize with me. On one end is your spirit. On the other end is your flesh. These are the two warring souls that are described in Romans 7. Who will win? In the middle is your mind, which is the regulator. Romans 12:2 says, "And do not be conformed to this world, but be transformed by the renewing of your mind, that you may prove what is that good and acceptable and perfect will of God."

The mind will make the final decision on who will win, your spirit or your flesh. If your mind is not renewed, and if you think two hours on Sunday out of 168 hours in a week will be enough to renew your mind, you are sadly mistaken. That's why so many Christians are still babes in Christ. It's even worse when Christians only attend church on Mother's Day, Easter, Father's Day, and Christmas.

Do you naively think that two hours on Sunday will be enough to ward off Satan's attacks via pornography, food commercials, flirtatious women, the latest gadget that costs more than you can afford? As our society is bombarded by seductive images and messages all day, every day via television, video games, radio, newspapers, magazines, and movies, unless our minds are renewed, we will not have the strength to stand against it all. Every day, Satan is throwing darts at you— thoughts, ideas, and suggestions. How often has this happened to you: you are enjoying your day, minding your own business, when all of a sudden a thought, an idea, a suggestion comes to you. This thought, idea, or suggestion seems to come from way out in left field, and it throws you completely off balance. You're driving, and suddenly you visualize yourself in an accident. You're walking down the street with your beloved mate. A woman passes by and suddenly you're imagining her in inappropriate ways.

If you know that your flesh and spirit are at war, then you will know that these thoughts are not your true thoughts. You do not have to own them. You can flick them off your spirit like lint on a coat. If you are actively growing in the knowledge of God, you will know that the enemy is out to destroy your life, and the things that you would never imagine on your own are weapons being hurled against you.

Your spirit man is the real you. For most people, even Christians, the body rules the spirit. This is not the way we were designed. We must strengthen our spirit through prayer, meditation, fasting, studying the Word, and hearing the Word. That way we can hear our Daddy's voice as separate and distinct from the enemy's, and our spirit man will rule the flesh. Strife will be eliminated, and we will achieve order and balance in our lives.

The Bible teaches us that we must cast out every imagination, every thought, that does not line up with the Word of God. In this war you need to ask yourself, was that a thought from Satan or was it from God? You will know it is from God if it lines up with His Word.

In the next chapter, A Masculine Jesus, we will look at the impact of Jesus' masculinity and image on the state of Black males.

CHAPTER 3: A MASCULINE JESUS

✝ Does your church empower or emasculate men?

✝ Do you dismiss or never discuss parts of the Bible where Jesus isn't nice?

✝ When wondering "WWJD," do you assume a gentle response?

✝ Do you think conflict and anger are sins?

✝ Are you the guy at church who never says no to an assignment, even if it diminishes other important aspects of your life?

✝ Do you think that being nice, observing etiquette, and knowingly allowing yourself to be used by others nevertheless leads people to salvation?

✝ Do you lack leadership in your family?

When you think of Jesus, what images come to mind? For many men, when they hear the word *Jesus,* they visualize a young, White male with blonde hair and blue eyes, who is weak, meek, soft, and on a cross, turning the other cheek. In the book, *What Color Was Jesus?,* we look at this question in detail.

Many elders have told me, "What difference does it make what color He is? Let's worship Him in spirit and in truth." I totally agree. But the mind is the regulator, and everything your mind has seen and heard is stored like a computer. If we are going to worship Him in spirit and in truth, then why do I see this White, blonde-haired, blue-eyed image on the window panes, church hand fans, Sunday school books, and the Cross? That image is not the truth!

Revelation 1:14–15 and Daniel 7:9 say that Jesus had hair the texture of wool and feet the color of bronze. Compare the Bible's description of Jesus with the image Pope Julius II had Michelangelo paint in 1505.

In Matthew 2:13, when Herod was looking for Jesus, Joseph hid his son in Egypt. I wonder how successful Joseph would have been hiding a White boy in Egypt.

I appreciate the elders' desire to worship Him in spirit and in truth, but the reality is, from a psychological perspective, it is difficult for the mind to go from a White image to no image instantaneously. It requires some transition, and I've been pleased to see that nationwide, many churches have been changing their images of Jesus Christ. It may be cost prohibitive to remove White images of Jesus from the window panes and stained glass, but we can start small by changing images on hand fans and Sunday school books.

THE RESURRECTION

Thank God, the story does not end on Good Friday on the Cross. A more masculine image of Jesus is His Resurrection.

One of the ways to empower men and make church more attractive is to present the image of a resurrected Jesus rather than a crucified Jesus. Or show both. There can be no Resurrection without a crucifixion.

The powerful movie directed by Mel Gibson, *The Passion*, graphically depicts that Jesus was not weak and a wimp. What He endured on the Cross was painful. Even when you read the four gospels, you do not get a full understanding of how painful it was to bear our sins on the Cross.

There have been some attempts to do so, but for all the graphic language that can be used, none is adequate. The pain of the Cross was all-consuming. Remember, Jesus was already a bloody pulp by the time He reached Golgotha. He had endured several mock trials. He had been scourged. The very flesh of His body lay open as the thongs of the flagella, impregnated with bone and lead, ripped at his naked frame. He had been mocked by the soldiers. A crown of thorns was woven and pressed hard upon His brow. He was beaten with a stick, spat upon, and struck with many blows. Then the Cross had been placed upon His back as He stumbled to make His way. He was at Calvary, stretched out upon the wooden, splintery Cross. Spikes were driven through his hands. His knees were bent, one foot placed over the other, and a large spike was driven through both. The Cross was then lowered into the ground. The torture had just begun.

Dying on a cross could be long and excruciating torture. The weight of the body would put great pressure on the medial nerves. Hanging there in that fashion would also cause the lungs to begin to fill up with fluid. Many people died from suffocation.

As the pain began to be unbearable, there was enough bend in the knee to push up for a breath of air and to relieve the pain in the arms. But that only caused more pain as the feet pushed bone against the metal spike. This literally could go on for hours.

Jesus endured all this physical suffering for us. You cannot imagine the agony He must have felt in His physical body as He hung there between heaven and earth.

The pain of the Cross extends even further. Mark 15:33–34:

A Masculine Jesus

"Now when the sixth hour had come, there was darkness over the whole land until the ninth hour. And at the ninth hour Jesus cried out with a loud voice, saying, 'Eloi, Eloi, lama sabachthani?'" which is translated, "My God, My God, why have You forsaken Me?"

He not only endured for us this physical pain, but He endured a separation from His Father.

How can we view Jesus as weak and feminine when He endured that much pain? If you think a 15-round match between Muhammad Ali and Joe Frazier was demanding, try going through what Jesus endured on the Cross. It is often said that if men had to give birth to children there would be no children, that the pain women have to endure during childbirth most men cannot bear to witness or experience. Childbirth is a pale comparison to the pain that Jesus endured on the Cross.

In order for the church to become more attractive to men, we need to talk about Jesus who was man enough to cry, tough enough to die, and strong enough to be resurrected. We need to make Jesus real. This is what men need.

What are we telling our 16-year-old sons who are being raised in church but have to walk through drug and gang infested neighborhoods on their way to school? Many boys have told me that their greatest challenge is not algebra, geometry, or trig, nor is it biology, chemistry, or physics. Their greatest challenge is the four-block walk from home to school.

What does the church say to this 16-year-old brother when the bullies want to take his money, possessions, and beat him up? Is he supposed to turn the other cheek? Let's look at this masculine Jesus and how He handled certain situations.

Matthew 21:12 says, "Then Jesus went into the temple of God and drove out all those who bought and sold in the temple, and overturned the tables of the money changers and the seats of those who sold doves."

JESUS TURNING OVER TABLES

Wait a minute. That does not sound like a meek, weak, and turning the other cheek Jesus. That's not how churches portray Jesus Christ. Matthew 21:12 does not say that Jesus politely requested the vendors to stop selling goods in His sanctuary or that He prayed for them or read scripture to them. It doesn't even say that He assigned His disciples the task of kicking the money changers out of the temple of God.

The scripture says *He* overturned the tables and chairs and drove them out on His own.

I never will forget. I was working in a church ministry and there was a disagreement in our rites of passage program about the role of physical development. I'm an advocate of physical development (martial arts, etc.). Christian men ought to be able to worship God and pray as well as do push ups and sit ups. I'm concerned about this idea that the church is filled with women and sissies. A sissy did not turn over that table and those chairs. A sissy did not drive those money changers from His sanctuary.

Ironically, some of the same churches that portray Jesus as weak, mild, and turning the other cheek retain a full security force. If you even think about taking any money from the basket when it's being passed around, believe me those security officers are not going to pray for you, they're not going to read scripture, they're not going to turn the other cheek, and they're not going to tell the pastor. They're going to take you out.

This masculine Jesus who overturned the tables and the chairs and drove them out was not overweight. He did not have a potbelly. He was not so weak that He could not overturn tables and chairs. It is obvious that He was in great shape. He was strong enough to fast for 40 days. Many of us could not fast for 40 minutes or 40 hours.

In John 10:18, this strong, masculine Jesus says that no one has the power to take His life. Even with His last breath on the Cross, He was clear and refused to compromise, even as He endured all that pain.

In Matthew 14:25, Jesus walked on water.

In Matthew 8:26, He spoke to the storm. He calmed the storm.

JESUS SPEAKING TO THE STORM

In John 2:7–9, He turned water into wine.

These images of Jesus Christ are not shown in church, so many men walk away because the weak, White, blonde-haired, blue-eyed image is simply not attractive to them. It's not attractive to most White men, much less Black men.

A Masculine Jesus

What are we going to tell this 16-year-old brother who is being preached at in church for two hours on Sunday but has to live the rest of the week dealing with the streets? How long will this brother survive turning the other cheek? Will he ever be able to keep his lunch money and Nike gym shoes? Will he live to see his 21st birthday? What are gangster rappers telling this brother? What is the Nation of Islam, specifically the Fruit of Islam, telling this brother?

Do our young boys join gangs for protection because the church has not provided any? In the Teenage Male Ministries chapter, I'll describe what one church did to provide protection for a school that was being overtaken by gangs.

Do you think this Jesus who did not allow money changers in His sanctuary would allow drug dealers and liquor stores in His neighborhood? Later, we'll also talk about a church that closed every one of the liquor stores in the surrounding neighborhood because the pastor and membership understood the power of Jesus Christ.

What does the church say to this 16-year-old brother? Let's have a conference where the youth are present, and we— the gangs, gangster rappers, the Fruit of Islam, and the church—will submit our proposals to them. Let's see whose answers will be acceptable to our young men.

Can you imagine a Black boy who not only knows Jesus, knows His Word, but also knows martial arts and regularly visits the health club? I can imagine him confidently telling the bullies and gang members, "Please don't mess with me, in the name of Jesus. It's in your best interest that you don't put a hand on me."

If the church is going to be attractive to Black men, specifically young Black men, Black men who feel the streets have the answer, we not only have to lift up this resurrected Jesus and emphasize what He did at His sanctuary, but we must tell the whole truth of what other men did in both the

Old and New Testaments when they were faced with adversity in their lives. John 18:1–10 reads:

"When Jesus had spoken these words, He went out with His disciples over the Brook Kidron, where there was a garden, which He and His disciples entered.

"And Judas, who betrayed Him, also knew the place; for Jesus often met there with His disciples.

"Then Judas, having received a detachment of troops, and officers from the chief priests and Pharisees, came there with lanterns, torches, and weapons.

"Jesus therefore, knowing all things that would come upon Him, went forward and said to them, 'Whom are you seeking?'

"They answered Him, 'Jesus of Nazareth.' Jesus said to them, 'I am He.' And Judas, who betrayed Him, also stood with them.

"Now when He said to them, 'I am He,' they drew back and fell to the ground.

"Then He asked them again, 'Whom are you seeking?' And they said, 'Jesus of Nazareth.'

"Jesus answered, 'I have told you that I am He. Therefore, if you seek Me, let these go their way,' that the saying might be fulfilled which He spoke, 'Of those whom You gave Me I have lost none.'

"Then Simon Peter, having a sword, drew it and struck the high priest's servant, and cut off his right ear."

Let's look at Peter. This was a bad brother. Peter reminds me of some security officers in the church: "We don't play that." Peter reminds me of the kind of officers we need in the church. In my earlier books, I've mentioned my concern about churches that use the Fruit of Islam to provide security. Do you see how ridiculous this is! Can you imagine the Fruit of Islam asking the church to protect their mosques?

A Masculine Jesus

What is it that the Fruit of Islam has that Christian men do not have? Does the Fruit of Islam walk around with weapons? No, they do not. Do they walk around fearful? No. The Bible clearly says in 2 Timothy 1:7, "For God has not given us a spirit of fear, but of power and of love and of a sound mind." I wonder how many men the church has lost because the church allowed the Fruit of Islam to protect them and the neighborhood.

There are more men in the church than in the Nation of Islam, so why is another group defending our own? Why aren't our own men stepping up to the plate?

Peter was a Christian, not a Muslim. He told his Savior, "We don't have to go out like this. I can take them out." Notice, Peter didn't call for his sword. It wasn't stored somewhere. He carried it. He used it on a regular basis or it would not have been with him. He did more than pull it out. He knew how to use it, and he cut the man's ear. These were the kind of brothers Jesus ran with.

We see yet another side of Peter in Matthew 14:25–29:

"Now in the fourth watch of the night Jesus went to them, walking on the sea.

"And when the disciples saw Him walking on the sea, they were troubled, saying, 'It is a ghost!' And they cried out for fear.

"But immediately Jesus spoke to them, saying, 'Be of good cheer! It is I; do not be afraid.'

"And Peter answered Him and said, 'Lord, if it is You, command me to come to You on the water.'

"So He said, 'Come.' And when Peter had come down out of the boat, he walked on the water to go to Jesus."

Now remember, Jesus spoke to all 12 disciples, but not all of them got out of the boat. Only Peter had the nerve to walk on water. There was something about Peter, and Jesus

29

knew it. Maybe that's why Peter was His right-hand man. In fact, when Jesus was resurrected and Mary saw Him, one of the first things that Jesus said was, "Go and tell Peter."

But Peter had his moments, and he at times lost the battle between flesh and spirit. Remember, it was Peter who betrayed Him—not once, not twice, but three times. Still, Jesus forgave His friend. We men need to meditate on these words. Jesus not only was tough enough to endure the Cross, He was man enough to forgive. Peter had betrayed Him three times, yet when Jesus rose, He wanted Peter to know that He forgave him and that Peter was one of the first persons He wanted to see.

If any man reading this book has a grudge with anyone, if there is any unforgiveness in your heart, you need to call that person and forgive.

Let me make it more personal. You will block the blessings of your life if you do not let go of the grudge you have for any person.

David

The Bible is full of men who were strong like Jesus. Let's talk about David in 1 Samuel 17. I encourage you to read this chapter in its entirety. The men of Israel were afraid of Goliath, but David, a teenage boy, knew that with God on his side, he could beat him. The men tried to convince David that there was no way to beat the giant. He was too tall, too strong. But David thought differently. This is the kind of man we need to portray in the church. When King Saul gave David his armor, bronze helmet, coat, and sword, David said, "I cannot walk with these for I have not tested them." David takes them off.

In 1 Samuel 17:34–37, David tells Saul,

"Your servant used to keep his father's sheep, and when a lion or a bear came and took a lamb out of the flock, I went out after it and struck it, and delivered the lamb from its mouth;

and when it arose against me, I caught it by its beard, and struck and killed it. Your servant has killed both lion and bear; and this uncircumcised Philistine will be like one of them, seeing he has defied the armies of the living God."

Then David says, "The Lord, who delivered me from the paw of the lion and from the paw of the bear, He will deliver me from the hand of this Philistine." Christians need to study the bear-killing, lion-wrestling, adultery-fleeing men of God. These are not weak images of manhood, and they can certainly stand up to bullies, gangs, gangster rappers, and social injustice.

Further into the story, Goliath says to David (verses 43–44), "'Am I a dog, that you come to me with sticks?' And the Philistine cursed David by his gods. And the Philistine said to David, 'Come to me, and I will give your flesh to the birds of the air and the beasts of the field!'" Clearly, Goliath didn't know who he was playing with. Bullies must learn that when they attempt to torment a child of the King, washed by the Blood and filled with the Holy Ghost, they are placing their own lives (and souls) in judgment.

What did David say (verses 45–46)?

"You come to me with a sword, with a spear, and with a javelin. But I come to you in the name of the Lord of hosts, the God of the armies of Israel, whom you have defied. This day the Lord will deliver you into my hand, and I will strike you and take your head from you. And this day I will give the carcasses of the camp of the Philistines to the birds of the air and the wild beasts of the earth, that all the earth may know that there is a God in Israel."

David proceeded to take him out, and a rock and a slingshot were all it took. This is what we need to tell the 16-year-old brothers who are being bullied by gangs.

Joshua and Caleb

Young Black males should also know about Joshua and Caleb. Read Numbers 13 for the complete, exciting story, but to summarize, the children of Israel were wandering in the wilderness. God told Moses to send 12 spies to Canaan, the Promised Land, on a secret military scouting mission to determine their strategy for invasion. Moses said (Numbers 13:17–20),

"Go up this way into the South, and go up to the mountains, and see what the land is like: whether the people who dwell in it are strong or weak, few or many; whether the land they dwell in is good or bad; whether the cities they inhabit are like camps or strongholds; whether the land is rich or poor; and whether there are forests there or not."

When they returned to base camp in the wilderness, ten of the spies gave Moses and the entire congregation a wimpish, weak report, saying, "They're giants and we're grasshoppers." Remember, death and life are in the power of the tongue. If you believe you are a grasshopper and the other team is better than your team, that he can run faster than you can, that they can fight better than you can, then they will win. As a man thinks in his heart, so is he. You will have what you say.

Ten out of 12, or 83 percent, of Moses' scouts returned from the mission too scared to fight. When they saw those giants, they panicked. This story reminds me of the church in Black America. We have 85,000 churches, sometimes three and four on a block. Despite this force, the church is still allowing liquor stores, crack houses, gang territories, alcohol billboards, and more to proliferate in our communities. These churches are only opened on Sundays from 11:00 to 1:00 and closed the rest of the week. It appears that the church has panicked in the presence of the giants of the underworld. We have a lot of entertainment churches that sing, dance, and shout, but where is the outreach into the streets? Where is the action?

Jesus was a man of action. The only time He sat down was to teach or pray, but mostly, He was on the move. He went to where the people were, even when it was dangerous to do so. And when the giants (the Sanhedrin) confronted Him, He went toe to toe with them. He had no fear. He did not sugarcoat His words, and He made no compromises. One of the major reasons many Black men do not go to church is because there are too many entertainment and containment churches in our neighborhoods. When this fearless, reaching-out Jesus becomes our role model, we will see more Black men in the church.

Joshua and Caleb were among the 12 spies Moses sent to Canaan. Unlike the other ten, they were not members of entertainment and containment churches. These two brothers symbolize the 17 percent of churches whose goal is liberation. In Numbers 13:30, Caleb said, "Let us go up at once and take possession for we are well able to overcome it." That's what we need to tell this young brother at the conference as he's being propositioned by the gangster rappers, gangs, and the Fruit of Islam. We—the church—are well able to overcome all the challenges that face him.

Gideon

I love the story of Gideon. He is a perfect man to study because he was so ordinary. Men want to be great but often secretly harbor feelings of unworthiness and low self-esteem that prevent them from taking action. Black men who are unemployed, in debt, dealing with family problems, etc., may feel unworthy to take on the problems in the community, but as the story of Gideon shows, one ordinary man can do extraordinary things when the spirit of God is on him.

Gideon's story is found in Judges, chapters six through nine. The story opens with Israel under Midianite rulership.

They suffered severe oppression because of their worship of foreign gods and their disobedience to God. They prayed to God for deliverance, and God sent them a prophet, who explained why God allowed the bondage to occur.

Enter Gideon. An angel appears to him as he's threshing wheat and says, "The Lord is with you, you mighty man of valor!" (Judges 6:12) Even though Gideon's family was poor in Manasseh and he considered himself the least in his father's house, the angel called him "a mighty man of valor." Brother, if someone called you a mighty man of valor, wouldn't you stand up straighter? Wouldn't you be able to see yourself as a strong, action-oriented man of God?

At first, Gideon was not convinced that he was the man for the job of going against an entire empire. He was just a simple brother from the hood who still lived at home with his father. He asked the angel to give him signs and proofs of his worthiness. Patiently, the angel proved that he indeed was a mighty man of valor. The truth is, God already knew Gideon was worthy. Gideon needed to know.

When Gideon was finally fully persuaded, he and an army of 300 "went up by the road of those who dwell in tents on the east of Nobah and Jogbehah; and he attacked the army while the camp felt secure. When Zebah and Zalmunna fled, he pursued them; and he took the two kings of Midian, Zebah and Zalmunna, and routed the whole army" (Judges 8:11–12).

With God and his angels on our side, we can take back our communities. We can empower our young men—even if only one strong man has the faith to stand for the Lord.

Pastors, ministers, and church officers, observe the young brothers in your church and community. Talk to them, listen to them. If you were a 16-year-old street brother, how would you answer the following questions:

Is the church in the neighborhood relevant? Would you join?

A Masculine Jesus

Does the church have ways to deal with the reality of the streets?

Does the church portray a masculine, strong image of Jesus Christ?

Is the decor of the church masculine?

Have you heard about what Jesus endured on the Cross and how He cleaned out His sanctuary?

Have you heard about Peter and his sword, David and Goliath, Joshua and Caleb, and Gideon?

Their answers will let you know if your ministries and outreach are being effective with young Black males.

CHAPTER 4: MALE TRENDS

In my books I often present statistics as a way of looking at conditions in our community. Usually these statistics are negative because of the many challenges facing us.

When I preach, men will often ask me to give them some good news about Black men. So first, I will present statistics that show the positive side of how Black men are succeeding in some major arenas, contrary to what we hear in the media day in and day out. These statistics may surprise you.

609,000+ African American males attend college. The media loves to talk about the large numbers of African American males who are involved with the penal system. They have been very quiet about the increasing numbers of African American males attending college. Each year we break the previous year's record. It would be nice if every once in a while the news would show African American males studying in college vs. the last drug deal and murder that went down.

400,000+ African American males are single parents. The media (especially talk shows) love to depict Black men as irresponsible, deadbeat fathers. Within the Black community we love talking about how strong Black women are and how they stay with their children and how weak the men are. It would be nice if every once in a while, the media and the Black community would lift up and acknowledge the 400,000+ African American males who are single-parent fathers. It would just bless my soul if on the news they would feature a Black male on Saturday night braiding his five-year-old daughter's hair in preparation for church on Sunday morning.

More than three million males are unashamed to call His name Jesus. Yes, we definitely want to increase the percentage of male attendance in church from 25 percent to at least 50 percent. While we are waiting and working to try and make that dream a reality, we need to acknowledge what the Lord has already done—more than three million men are unashamed to call His name Jesus.

That's the good news. Now let's look at the challenges.

Forty-five percent of African American women will *never* marry due to the male shortage. Many women will marry, but it will not last. The African American divorce rate is 66 percent. The solution to the male shortage is not for the few available men to practice serial monogamy. We need male ministries to develop boys into responsible God loving men, husbands, and fathers.

I mentioned earlier that one of every three African American males are involved with the penal system. There are close to one million Black males who are involved in federal, state, and local penal institutions. Close to 500,000 are either on probation or house arrest. Satan projects that by the year 2020, two of every three African American males will be involved with the penal system.

Fourteen percent of all African American males are disenfranchised, and some of them, depending on the state, have been permanently disenfranchised. Is this the same United States of America that goes abroad to other countries, insisting that they convert to a democratic form of government? America promotes democracy and has had us in numerous wars to enforce a changeover, yet look at what we do at home. Fourteen percent of African American males are not allowed the right to vote because of their involvement with the penal system. We could have won numerous local, state, and national elections if only our men could have voted.

There are 300,000 African American males released from prison annually, many of them victims of "bootie raids" in prison. The majority of them are released, but not tested. We are living with walking timebombs in our community. Forty-five percent of all men in America that are AIDS infected are African American. This travesty at least partially explains why 68 percent of all women in America with AIDS are African American. More will be said about this in the AIDS ministries chapter.

Incarcerated men face many of the same challenges, including illiteracy, fatherlessness, and no church home. Many lack a high school diploma, and many, when taken by the police, were on some corner between 10:00 pm and 3:00 am.

African American boys are 8 percent of public school children, but they constitute 33 percent of the students placed in special education or suspension. Is there a relationship between special education and prison? Between illiteracy and incarceration? Between Ritalin and crack cocaine?

Has special education become the new form of tracking? Why is it that girls, specifically White girls, are placed in special education the least and African American males the most?

Depending on the city, the school dropout rate for African American males is between 20 and 80 percent. Yes, in some cities the dropout rate is as high as 80 percent! One of every 10 African American male high-school students lives in New York or Chicago and they have the highest dropout rate after Baltimore. If we just concentrated in these two or three cities, much of our problem would be solved.

Pastors and ministers should visit their local school(s) and demand that the administration provide an accurate dropout rate. (Some schools take credit when a student earns his high school diploma via a GED. Clearly, this is cheating.) The best way to measure the dropout rate is to look at those students who entered the school as freshmen and to monitor whether those students graduated.

Can we accept a dropout rate of almost 50 percent in most urban areas? Can you imagine that most school superintendents are cognizant that 50 percent of their students who enter kindergarten will not graduate? How can we rationalize spending almost $7,000 per year per student with a performance like that?

Is it true that governors determine prison growth based on fourth grade reading levels? Wouldn't a better response be to improve schools, curricula, and pedagogy than to increase the prison budget, especially with the prison system's recidivism rate of 85 percent?

If we're trying to balance the budget, isn't Head Start, Title 1, Pell Grants, and job training more cost effective than prisons? Why are we spending $28,000 per inmate per year with a recidivism rate of 85 percent?

Could it be that prisons are built in the rural parts of states to employ poor White males who can't find jobs anywhere else? Is that why we build prisons while cutting Head Start, Title 1, and Pell Grants?

Another alarming statistic has to do with male unemployment. The Labor Department states that Black male unemployment is at 11 percent. In New York, a study done by some university officials puts the figure closer to 50 percent. Can you imagine in New York City that 50 percent of adult Black males are unemployed? Do you know how difficult it is to live in a patriarchal, capitalistic country without employment? Before God gave Adam Eve, God gave Adam a job. He was a zoologist. His job was to name and classify the animals. The Bible says that if a man does not work, he does not eat.

With its 85,000 churches, $50 billion in assets, and $3 billion in annual revenues, does the church have any answers to this unemployment problem?

How many African American males has your ministry employed?

For young Black males between the ages of 16 and 35, it all boils down to economics.

Male Trends

Fatherlessness

The following is a historical snapshot of African American fathers present in the home:

- 1920 – 90 percent
- 1960 – 80 percent
- 2006 – 32 percent

The declining presence of Black fathers in the home provides a major clue to the question, What happened to the Black family?

Some say that slavery caused the decline of the Black family. Didn't slavery end in 1865? Fifty-five years after slavery ended, that is, in 1920, 90 percent of Black youth had their fathers in the home compared to 32 percent today. Slavery cannot explain fatherlessness in the Black community.

Some say the Black family was hit hard by the Industrial Revolution. When America moved from the farm in the South to manufacturing in the North —the Great Migration—that was the death knell of the Black family. The Great Migration occurred between 1910 and the early 1920s. There was still a high percentage of fathers in the home, so that cannot explain what happened.

So what did happen between 1960 and 2006? I thought slavery was one of Satan's best tricks, but what slavery did not do to the Black family has been done by crack cocaine and welfare. America is trying its best to send every brother to jail that is in possession of five grams of crack. The government has tried to destroy the Black family by removing the man and by providing welfare to women.

More than 60 percent of the brothers who are incarcerated are in prison because of crack cocaine. Later in the book we will look at developing strong ministries related to prison and drugs. Knowing that substance abuse has been a destructive weapon against healthy, intact Black families, the church must step up to the plate and provide strong ministries for prisons, drug abuse, and family restoration.

When fathers are not in the home, children are at risk:

- 63 percent of youth that commit suicide are from fatherless homes.
- 90 percent of all homeless and runaway children are from fatherless homes.
- 85 percent of all children that exhibit behavioral disorders come from fatherless homes.
- 80 percent of rapists motivated by displaced anger come from fatherless homes.
- 71 percent of all high school dropouts come from fatherless homes.
- 75 percent of all adolescent patients in chemical abuse centers come from fatherless homes.
- 70 percent of juveniles in state-operated institutions come from fatherless homes.
- 85 percent of all youth sitting in prison grew up in fatherless homes.
- 82 percent of teenage girls who get pregnant come from fatherless homes.[1]

I believe the Black community is experiencing God's wrath because God is not pleased with fathers not assuming responsibility for their children and families.

The church must understand how Black men are responding to the challenge of fatherhood and educate and minister to them with a strong sense of urgency. There are several types of fathers:

1. Sperm Donors
2. No Show Daddies
3. Ice Cream Daddies
4. Stepfathers
5. Daddies
6. Divorced Daddies

Male Trends

Sperm Donors don't stay long, only about 18 seconds. There are many sperm donors in Black America. Fathering is a marathon, not a sprint. It takes 18 years, not 18 seconds, to raise a child.

No Show Daddies promise to pick the child up, but they seldom show. Imagine what it's like for a child to be excited about daddy coming to pick him up, but he never shows. Can we blame that on the White man too? I don't think so.

Now I have a gag order to mothers: if you have a problem with your ex, that's between you and your ex. It may be tempting, but resist the urge to run your negative agenda through your child. Putting down the father in front of the child hurts him even more.

Ice Cream Daddies show up, buy the kids ice cream, take them to the baseball game, football game, basketball game, to an amusement park—whereever the child wants to go. But they are weak when it comes to helping the child do homework, enforcing chores, and other responsibilities. Children love Ice Cream Daddies. They love to play their Ice Cream Daddies against their mothers.

Then we have **Stepdads**. I hate that term. How can a man who stays, pays the bills, checks homework, and puts food on the table be called a stepfather when a Sperm Donor is called a father? Something is wrong with this picture.

And then we have the real thing, the real man. We have **Daddies**. Dads stay 18 years and longer. They know that in order to develop a male from a boy to a man will not only take nurturance, it will require God's wisdom.

Many men who want to be real Daddies have told me, "I'm a **divorced dad**. I want to spend time with my child, but the mother makes it difficult. The courts are tough on me when it comes to paying child support, but they do not enforce my visits with the child." It is not fair, but as a man of God and a

Daddy who is trying to do the right thing, you must continue to fight for the right to be with your child. Never give up. They need you, and you need them.

Which type of man are you?

Recently, the journal *Nature* described a South African study of young elephants raised in a herd that had lost all adult male members. These fatherless juveniles were easily agitated. They became wild and destructive, killing and causing chaos at random. This is not typical elephant behavior, and destroying these violent youngsters seemed a likely option. The wildlife managers captured the young beasts and shipped them off to a herd with a healthy population of adult males. The results were dramatic. The young elephants settled down as the older males began to imprint "correct male elephant behavior" onto them.[2]

Why Some Black Boys Don't Believe They Need Men in Their Lives

❖ It is difficult to admit that you need someone whom you have never (or seldom) experienced.

❖ They have never experienced a man in authority.

❖ Their mother told them that they were the *man of the house*.

❖ If they are the man of the house, they do not need, nor value a male teacher, counselor, dean, administrator, coach, mentor, or any other male in authority.

Male Trends

❖ They do not need a man to provide, because their mother is the provider.

❖ They do not need a man to teach them how to farm or work in a factory, because those jobs are obsolete.

❖ They do not need a man to teach them how to develop skills in the area of information systems, because either a woman can do that, or they do not value those skills.

❖ They do not need a man to teach them about sexuality, because they "think" that *life* has adequately educated them.

❖ They do not need a man to teach them how to rap, play basketball, or fight, because their friends can teach them.

❖ They do not need a man to teach them how to drive, because schools provide drivers education classes.

❖ They do not need a man to teach them how to repair things, because America has decided that it's cheaper to just discard the old and purchase the new (all from overseas.)

❖ They do not need a man to teach them how to treat a lady because certain media, as well as their peers, have them believing that the female doesn't desire or deserve to be treated with respect.

❖ They do not need a man to teach them how to be a father because they "unknowingly" have decided to be a sperm donor.

❖ Finally, because their mother appointed them the *man of the house*, they may never have a need to leave!

A final thought: before you get involved in your church's ministries, you must attend to your number one ministry, and that is raising your children, providing for your family, and serving as priest in the home. Malachi 4:6 reads:

"And he will turn
 The hearts of the fathers to the children,
 And the hearts of the children to their fathers,
 Lest I come and strike the earth with a curse."

And then there was silence for 400 years before we heard anything from the Lord in the New Testament. God is serious about fatherhood. He is concerned about the father being in his rightful place, not only as provider, but as priest of the home. When the father is not in place, mothers and children are displaced.

In the next chapter, we will revisit my earlier book, *Adam, Where Are You?* and find out exactly the state of Adam in the church.

CHAPTER 5: ADAM UPDATE

In 1994, I wrote the bestseller *Adam, Where Are You? Why Most Black Men Don't Go to Church.* There has been a tremendous response to this book. It has been used in numerous Bible studies, retreats, seminars, and conferences. In this chapter, I will revisit that question with more than a decade of additional wisdom and experience.

I felt it was necessary to revisit the 21 reasons that explain why most churches have less than 40 percent male membership. The 21 reasons are as follows (listed in no particular order):

1. Hypocrisy
2. Ego/dictatorial
3. Faith/submission/trust/forgiveness/anger
4. Passivity
5. Tithing
6. Irrelevance
7. Eurocentric
8. Length of service
9. Emotional
10. Sports
11. Attire/dress code
12. Classism/unemployment
13. Education/literacy
14. Sexuality and drugs
15. Homosexuality
16. Spirituality/universalism/worshipping alone
17. Heaven
18. Evangelism
19. Lack of Christian role models
20. Streets/peer pressure
21. Double standards/forced on a child

Before I review some of the above reasons, let me mention that within almost every institution—colleges, corporate America, families, public schools, teachers—there is a shortage of Black men. The church is not alone. Black women have a shortage of Black men to choose from. Principals have a shortage of Black male teachers to choose from. College presidents have a shortage of Black male college students to choose from. Corporate America has a shortage of African American males to choose from. The list is endless. The church is not alone.

There are a few institutions that have an adequate supply of Black men, however. They include jails and prisons, nightclubs, the corner, health clubs, bowling alleys, and basketball courts.

If you want to find out where Black men are on Sunday morning at 11:00 am, all you have to do is drive through the community and go to the basketball court. You'll see a court full of brothers when church is in session. You can also find them on the tennis court, the golf course, the softball diamond, the health club, and the bowling alley. Ironically, the best leagues in the city play at Sunday morning at 11:00 am.

Interestingly, these same brothers who have a problem with tithing don't have a problem spending $50 to $100 on their weekly bowling and poker games.

Many brothers are at work on Sunday morning at 11:00 am. These are good men, blue collar workers who unfortunately work a shift that prevents them from being in the house of the Lord on Sunday morning at 11:00 am.

Many brothers choose to work around their house. They are excellent providers, good fathers, but rather than praising our Lord and Savior Jesus Christ, they choose to cut the grass, wash the car, paint the house, and make repairs.

I have been asked numerous times what I think are the two or three major reasons that explain why Adam is not in church. Simply, I believe the major reason why Black men do not go to church is lack of faith. Hebrews 11:6 says, "But without faith it is impossible to please Him, for he who comes to God must believe that He is, and that He is a rewarder of those who diligently seek Him."

To have a personal relationship with Jesus requires faith. In our world, which is carnal, secular, visual, and concrete, it is difficult for men to believe in someone they have not seen.

Have you ever seen your brain? Do you believe you have one? Even though most people have not seen their brain, they know they have one. Even though I have never seen God, I know He exists. I do not need to see Him to believe in Him.

1 Corinthians 2:14 says, "But the natural man does not receive the things of the Spirit of God, for they are foolishness to him; nor can he know *them*, because they are spiritually discerned."

Believing in God requires spiritual discernment. The natural man cannot discern the spirit. The natural man has to see it, taste it, smell it, touch it, and hear it, but faith does not use or require the five senses.

One of the greatest challenges facing the church is finding creative ways to attract men. Man does not live by bread, or his flesh, alone. But men who are still in the world do not know that their soul hungers for more than the next fix—sex, food, drugs, television, whatever it may be. So we must meet them at their point of need first before giving them the Word of God.

We must feed them, house them, and provide them clothing. When they ask, "Why did you do that for me?" then we can share with them the love of our Savior Jesus Christ. Because we fed them and met them at their point of need, they are more willing to listen to us talk about our Lord and Savior who motivated us to help them.

The same is true when we are trying to attract men to the church. Throughout these pages I have addressed this question of what men need. If the church seriously looks at the needs of Black men and addresses those issues head on, then men may be more willing to hear us talk about our God.

The Bible reminds us in James 2:26: "For as the body without the spirit is dead, so faith without works is dead also." Many men question our faith because they have seen so few tangible works by the church. The community is still suffering from poor health care, crime, violence, unemployment—the list goes on. They are asking the church, what have you done for me lately?

My pastor, Bill Winston (Living Word Christian Center) once spoke to a group of young males in a high school. They were not interested in listening to a pastor, and they initially tuned him out. But when he talked about moving from a storefront church to a mall that provides more than 1,000 jobs, the young brothers perked up. They became interested in hearing about not only the mall and the jobs, but his God.

The second major reason why Black men don't go to church is because of hypocrisy. Everyone, especially brothers, wonders how four churches on a block can have a liquor store and a crack house for neighbors. Churches should be making a difference, not accepting the status quo.

Another hypocrisy brothers will tell you about is that the pastors they used to run with in their youth—are still running with them on Saturday night.

Many brothers wonder if the only institution Black men can run are churches. Why is it in White communities you see large numbers of businesses and a sprinkling of churches, but in the Black community it's the reverse—a large number of ineffective churches and a sprinkling of businesses, primarily barbershops, hair salons, nail salons, barbeque shops, and fast food restaurants?

Some brothers believe you have to have your act together to go to church, that the church is a museum for saints rather than a hospital for sinners or a school for students. Those who feel this way will never feel worthy enough to go to church. I wonder where they got that notion. From other church members?

This is why evangelism is so important. We must walk the streets and create a dialogue with brothers. We need to tell them our stories. We need to tell them where we were and how we still struggle. We need to describe the struggle that Paul so eloquently writes about in Romans 7:24: "Oh wretched man that I am!"

Entertainment and containment churches believe that they have the answers and you have to come inside their facilities to find them. If we operate from that premise, large numbers of Black males may never come to church. Liberation churches, on the other hand, understand the importance of evangelism and dialogue. It is important to go out and listen to the needs of the people.

Does your church have an evangelism team?

How important is evangelism in your church?

Does the pulpit make evangelism important?

Does the budget reflect evangelism activities?

Are your members encouraged to evangelize?

Are they trained to evangelize effectively?

Although all of the 21 reasons mentioned above are significant, I must highlight tithing, offerings, and money that is given to the church. One of the major needs of Black men is money. It is difficult, if not impossible, to function without capital in this country. Brothers have a major problem giving capital to someone they feel is a hypocrite and to a God they cannot see.

Earlier we mentioned that at best 26 percent of Christians are tithers, at worst, only 4 percent. So it's not just Black men that have a problem giving to the church. People in the church, who holler and shout, may only give a dollar when the basket comes around.

You've heard the classic story between the $1 bill and the $20 bill. The $20 bill says, "I've been around the world.

I've been to the best hotels. I've been on cruises. I've been to the Bahamas, Bermuda, and Hawaii. I have enjoyed myself in some of the finest restaurants on earth."

The $1 bill is jealous. He says, "You mean you've been to all those places and done those things? I've been locked in church all of my life. These church members don't want to let me go."

I've met numerous men who tell me they believe in God but are not inclined to worship. They'd rather believe in God at home and keep their money to themselves. The Bible reminds us that we should not forsake the assembling of one to another and we are to encourage one another.

For a secular, carnal person who's having difficulties paying his bills, it's difficult to believe that tithing 10 percent to God or the church will help him. He believes it is better to keep the 100 percent, especially when he has cash flow problems.

If you have $1,000 worth of bills and $900 in income, from a carnal perspective, it makes no sense to give 10 percent of your income because this would exacerbate your cash flow problems. But from a faith perspective, it is actually better to give God 10 percent or more and live off the 90 percent or less.

I enjoyed reading David Murrow's book, *Why Men Hate Going to Church.* He looks at men of all races. Let me share some of Murrow's positions:

"Men who express an interest in art or religion were more likely to answer like a woman than other men. Interest in religion or art is a mark of definitely greater femininity than lack of interest in these matters. Most masculine of all are the men who have little or no interest in religion. Very masculine men show little interest in religion, very feminine men, great interest. Young men, athletic men, and uneducated men tended to be more consistently masculine than old men, sedentary men, and educated men." [3]

Adam Update

At the outset of this book I said that my heart is primarily with 12 to 35-year-old African American males. These males are in their prime. For the church to remain viable in the future, it must do a better job of attracting these men. The church cannot grow with only women, girls, and elderly men.

Is it true that men who are athletically inclined and undereducated are least interested in church? What is it about the church that is unattractive to these men? Why is the church more attractive to elderly, sedentary, and educated men?

In my earlier books—*Countering the Conspiracy to Destroy Black Boys* and *Keeping Black Boys Out of Special Education*—I spend an endless amount of time addressing the miseducation of our boys. Eighty percent of special education students should not have been placed there. They should have been given classes in remedial reading.

Being able to read is a critical aspect of most church services. Imagine being illiterate and attending a worship service. You cannot fully participate in the worship service when the minister says, "Let's read the announcements in the bulletin" or "Let's open your hymnals to page 100 and sing together."

In the mega-churches, the lyrics are shown throughout the sanctuary on screens and monitors. This is just as problematic. When the pastor refers you to a particular passage in the Bible, if you are illiterate, there is no way you can read along or move from one book or one verse to another. (Heaven forbid if you're looking for a verse in Zephaniah followed by a verse in Zachariah.)

It is tragic for a Black boy to be in ninth grade with a third grade reading level or for a Black man to be 25 years old and illiterate. Churches must address the root issue, which is the miseducation of our children in school. Until illiteracy is completely eradicated from our community, churches should be more sensitive about having the congregation read aloud and sing from hymnals. We should make the Bible available on audiocassette tapes and CDs. If Black youth can memorize the lyrics of a rap tune without reading, that lets us know that the oral tradition is a viable way to teach those who are illiterate the Word of God.

Men love technology, yet many churches are still operating as if they are in the 19th century. We need to move the church into the 21st century. With technology changing so rapidly, the church should be on the cutting edge of this movement. We should involve men in this changing technology.

In my book *Keeping Black Boys Out of Special Education,* I address the fact that almost 80 percent of African American children placed in special education are male because many teachers are not cognizant of gender learning differences. Researchers theorize that boys have a shorter attention span because they produce less serotonin than girls. Given this aspect of male physiology, teachers should either shorten the lesson or gear it more toward male interests. The same applies to pastors. If you know that males have a shorter attention span, then the sermon needs to be shortened.

Thom and Joani Schultz discovered the following about sermons:

- 12 percent say they usually remember the message.
- 87 percent say their minds wandered during the sermons.
- 35 percent say the sermons are too long.
- 11 percent of women and 5 percent of men credit sermons as their primary source of knowledge about God.[4]

Unfortunately, we are living in an era where people are having a difficult time focusing and the attention span is declining. Television has contributed to the decline. Images quickly change every one to one-and-one-half seconds. Information is presented in six to eight-minute blocks, which are followed by commercials.

Adam Update

Those of you who went to church this past Sunday—do you remember what the sermon was about? Test your memory the moment you walk out of church, again after dinner, and again Monday morning. Chances are, unless you make a concerted effort to remember, the pastor's words will be like clouds disappearing in the wind.

Yet pastors continue to believe sermons are the best way to teach the Word of God. Well, if you keep doing what you've been doing and expect a different outcome, that borders on insanity. If only 12 percent of the congregation remembers the sermon, 87 percent say their minds wander, 35 percent say the sermons are too long, and only 5 percent of men credit sermons as their primary source of knowledge, is this really the best way to teach the Word of God?

Let's look at how Jesus taught and preached. He taught through three methods: storytelling, miracles, and meeting the needs of people.

How long were Jesus' sermons? I do not know, but He did know how to tell a good story, and storytelling is a highly effective way to help people remember information. Jesus taught in parables. In my opinion, He was the greatest storyteller that ever lived.

The second and third methods really go together. Jesus taught with miracles, and he met the people at their point of need. If someone needed healing, He healed them. If someone was mentally deranged, He cast out the demons. When Jesus' disciples saw all those hungry people—5,000 men plus their wives and children—they wanted to turn them away. But Jesus met them at their point of need. With five loaves and two fish, He fed them all. The miracle was the sermon.

When you heal a man, employ, and feed him, he may be able to hear more than six to eight minutes of a sermon because now you have his full attention. He's no longer sick or worried about the bills stacking up or so hungry he can't think. His needs have been met.

I'm concerned about praise and worship. Visualize young brothers 12 to 35 years old in church, street brothers, hard brothers being asked to hold hands and sing. That may be problematic for some of them. In many churches, the singing of hymns is often led by women. It is difficult for brothers with baritone and bass voices to feel comfortable singing in the high ranges.

Murrow offers the following:

"Even among churchgoers, singing is more popular with women than men. We polled our 1,500-member church. While three-quarters of the women chose praise singing as a top priority, about half the guys chose it. Robert Lewis has noticed a curious trend at his Arkansas mega-church: praise skippers. These people, mostly men, consistently arrive half an hour late to the worship service. Lewis suspects these fellows are tardy on purpose to miss the singing. I'm convinced that there are a million unchurched men who would attend a worship service this weekend if they just didn't have to sing. Pastor Lewis dropped singing from his men's fraternity gatherings and attendance leaped. Some church planner is going to figure this out and reap a rich harvest of men."[5]

If you keep doing what you've been doing and expecting a different outcome, it borders on insanity. We need to step back a moment and do some market research. If we ascertained that there are people, especially males in the 12-to 35-year-old range, who do not want to hold hands or be led by a praise team singing in a soprano or alto voice, we may need to change our worship service.

Why don't Black men go to church? "Cuz they been!" Now let's think about this. Just because large numbers of men don't go to church doesn't mean they have never been to church. Most have been to church at least once. They are aware of what goes on in church. They have made a conscious decision, not based on lack of information, but because of what they experienced in church. They have decided that church is not the place they want to attend.

Men love women. Men like looking at women. Men like being with women. So you would think if the church is filled with women, if for no other reason, men would attend church just to be around women. Not true. Not even a church filled with women is reason enough to attend.

I'm concerned about Adam Sr. and am even more concerned about Adam Jr. African American males between 12 and 19 years old cause the greatest havoc in our community and are the least represented in church. In researching my book *Hip Hop: A Street Curriculum,* I immersed myself in rap and the impact on youth. Later, in the Teenage Male Ministries chapter, we will look at this in more detail. For now I'll simply ask, Is 50 Cent raising our children? Do rappers have a greater influence on our youth than the church? Do we design the worship service for the 65-year-old female or the 16-year-old brother?

Pastors and church leaders, imagine yourself as a 16-year-old Black male, sitting through your worship service. Honestly, is the service appealing enough to make this young Black male want to attend church? Adolescents are important to the lifeblood of the church. Now they may be going to church because a parent (mama) makes them, but in a year or two, they will be adults and on their own. Will they come to your church when mama no longer has a say? Will they come to church voluntarily and on their own?

I pray that church leaders have not become like politicians who respond to the constituencies that give the most money. Have we designed a worship service for 65-year-old females because they represent the largest component of church members? According to David Murrow,

"In most churches women's ministry is the church's top priority. One day I was browsing a catalogue of ministry offerings at a large church. This congregation offered eight pages of ministry to and for women: women's Bible study, women's prayer circle, women's retreat, women's tea, women's support groups, on and on. The men's ministry page offered two options: a monthly men's breakfast and an annual retreat. This church had two full-time ministers to women but no ministers to men. Why the huge disparity? Probably because women sign up for things and men don't. Nevertheless, this eight to one ratio of ministry offerings sends a powerful message to men. Church is for women, not for you."[6]

This reminds me of athletic departments where the football and basketball programs literally finance the other sports programs. In many churches, the women's ministries finance the other components of the church. Consequently, many pastors know that in order for the church to remain financially stable, the women's ministries must remain strong, unfortunately to the detriment of ministries and budgets geared toward young African American men.

Pastor, what percent of your budget is allocated to youth? What percentage of church space (square footage) is allocated to youth? What percentage of your ministries is allocated to youth? If less than 10 percent of your budget, space, and ministries are allocated to youth, then youth are not a priority in your church. In the Teenage Male Ministries chapter, we will look at an excellent institutional role model, Allen A.M.E. Church pastored by Floyd Flake. This ministry takes young people seriously, and you can see it not only in the budget but in the space allocated for youth.

I've had the privilege of preaching at Allen A.M.E. numerous times, and every time Pastor Flake makes it clear to me that I have to preach to both adults and youth. Can you imagine, each ministry, adults and youth, having its own separate sanctuary! They have a worship service exclusively geared to youth called Shekinah. Can you imagine hundreds of youth worshipping Jesus in rap, drama, stepping, dance, choirs, poetry, scripture, prayer, and sermons all led by youth. The youth feel important at Allen A.M.E. Do youth feel important in your church?

As a consultant to schools, I have recommended for the past two decades single gender classrooms. Research shows an improvement in test scores and grade point averages and a reduction in special education and suspensions. I now recommend this for Sunday School. Adam Jr. needs a new experience. He needs a male teacher who will understand his different learning styles while teaching him to love Jesus.

Sunday School should not be a continuation of regular school. Most boys are bored with the curriculum and disdain being taught with textbooks, ditto sheets, and boring lectures. Let's make Sunday School exciting for boys. If Adam Jr. loves Sunday school, he will stay in church the rest of his life.

One of the major reasons why Adam is not in church is because men believe they have resolved the major issues posed in John 3:16 and Romans 10:9. Many men will tell you they believe in God. They will say they are saved. If you ask them when they got saved, they will say it was some time during their childhood. Their mother took them to church, and walked them down the aisle. They recited John 3:16 and confessed Romans 10:9—and that was more than 30 years ago. At funerals, the minister will often say that the deceased accepted Christ at an early age. Let me translate. The mama walked him down the aisle, he gave his life to Christ, and lying here in the casket is the first time he's been to church in 30 years.

Another classic statement is "once saved, always saved." I've never seen that statement in the Bible. I have seen Matthew 7:23: "I never knew you; depart from Me, you who practice lawlessness!"

Romans 10:9 says, "If you confess with your mouth the Lord Jesus and believe in your heart that God has raised Him from the dead, you will be saved." Becoming saved requires not only a confession by mouth, it requires a belief in your heart.

Many men who are convinced of their salvation believe they have the Golden Insurance Card. "I know I'm going to heaven because of what I did 30 years ago when my mama walked me down the aisle. So if I'm supposed to go to church to secure eternal life, I resolved that 30 years ago. Therefore there's no need to go to church. I need to spend the rest of my life trying to get some money."

According to pollster George Barna, when it comes to the way we live our lives, there's not much difference between those who claim to be believers and those who don't.

This is just what most men suspect. People who go to church are just as good or just as lousy as people who don't. So why bother wasting time with something that makes no obvious difference one way or the other?

To the shame of the church, the kind of Christianity we've demonstrated has often not been convincing enough to attract men toward it.

Consider these statistics the Barna Research Group came up with about areas of vital importance to the Christian faith.

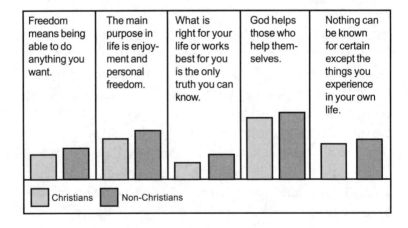

Adam Update

Note how the rate of agreement with these statements is nearly a dead heat between believers and nonbelievers. Christians get divorced at the same rate as unbelievers, hold the same values as unbelievers, and think in much the same ways as unbelievers. Barna delivers this biting summary: "After studying 131 different indicators of who we are as people, we concluded that it is difficult for non-Christians to understand Christianity since few born-again individuals model a biblical faith."

So why would a man find it necessary to go to church? Men are generally pragmatic and practical. They're problem solvers and solution finders. Many men see church as a bland, lukewarm society with no real relevance or agenda. If involvement in a church makes no functional difference in the quality of life—if it does not challenge, invigorate, or empower a man—why attend?[7]

What they have not resolved is how to live their lives victoriously. Going to church is like going to school. Not only do we go to church to get saved and resolve the eternal heaven question, we go to learn how to live a better life. We go to learn about all the gifts, rights, and blessings God has for us. We go to church to improve our relationship with God by studying His Word. We learn how to bind demons and speak correctly. We learn about our rights at church. John 3:2 teaches, "Beloved, I pray that you may prosper in all things and be in health, just as your soul prospers."

A good church will teach you that you have a right to be healthy. You have a right to a good marriage. You have a right to live prosperously, but only as your soul prospers. If men continue to see hypocrites live one way Monday through Saturday and another way on Sunday, then they won't see a need to go to church. But if they see Christians trying their best to live what they learn on Sundays, and actually producing good fruit, then men will become curious and give it a chance.

It's a sad commentary when no one on your job or in your school knows you're saved. There should be something different about you, a Christian. When you walk into a room, people immediately should know there's something different about you. They should know soon that you are a Christian and to not curse around you. Certain topics should never come up in your presence. When I walk into the barbershop, the conversation changes. A Christian has walked into the barbershop, and while I am there, no bragging about female conquests, how many babies they made, etc.

In the next chapter we will look at what men need. You can't develop strong male ministries until you first develop strong men.

CHAPTER 6:
WHAT MEN NEED

Is a sports partner your friend?

Is a former classmate your friend?

Is a military buddy your friend?

Who is your closest male friend? How frequently do you communicate with him? Does he know your most intimate secrets?

Do you know your best friend's birthday? What did you give him?

Are you secure with your friend?

What do you like about him?

What is true manliness?

What is success?

How do you deal with guilt feelings?

What is integrity?

Have you been with a woman in an inappropriate way this week? Could it have looked to others that you were using poor judgment?

Have you been completely above reproach in all your financial dealings this week?

Have you exposed yourself to any explicit material this week?

Have you spent daily time in prayer and in the scriptures this week?

Have you fulfilled the mandate of your calling this week?

Have you taken time off to be with your family this week?

Have you just lied to me?

It is amazing how different men are from women. For example, in a restaurant, there are two couples. One of the ladies tells the other lady, "Come go with me to the rest room," and they will continue to talk. You can count the times that a man will tell another man, "Come go with me to the rest room so we can continue our conversation."

A father will ask his children when they come home from school, "How was school today?" and the children will say, "It was okay." When the mother asks the same question, however, the children will give a complete 30-minute report of their day, period by period, hour by hour.

There are men who are going through a divorce, and no one knows. Unemployed, and no one knows. Laid off their job, and no one knows. Suffering with cancer, and no one knows.

Men need close male friends with whom they can share their most intimate secrets, fears, desires, concerns, and goals. This trusted friend must be chosen with care. I play tennis, but it does not mean that my tennis partners are my friends. We may play hours of tennis together, but that does not mean I feel comfortable sharing personal information with them.

Most women know their friends' birthdays, and they will call, send a card, gift, or some other form of acknowledgment. Do you know your best friend's birthday? Did you do anything for him on his birthday?

Men commit suicide because they hold things inside much more than they should. I have used the questions listed at the beginning of the chapter in numerous retreats with men, and it always amazes me the stories and insights that pour out. When we are honest and share with one another, we will find out how great we really are.

The following are the keys to a man's soul:
1. His goals—what he wants most in life
2. His thoughts—what he thinks about most of the time
3. His finances—how he spends his money
4. His pursuits—how he spends his leisure time
5. His friends—the people with whom he associates

What Men Need

6. His attention—who and what he admires and appreciates
7. His humor—what amuses him

What are your goals? What are your 5, 10, 15, 20, 30 year plans? What do you think about more than any other thought?

If I looked at your checkbook, what would I see? Does your checkbook reflect your priorities? Many brothers spend more for their cars than their residence. How can the car note exceed the rent or mortgage?

How do you spend your leisure time? If you want to find out where brothers are Sunday at 11:00 am, consider visiting the basketball court, the bowling alley, softball diamond, golf course, or health club. In the book *The Man in the Mirror,* Patrick Morley shares the following observations about men:

"I want to make a difference.

I want to make life count.

I want my life to have meaning.

I want to have an impact.

I want to make a contribution.

I want to do something important with my life.

I want to conquer, achieve, excel, prove myself.

I want to be somebody.

I want my life to be significant."

Women want to be heard because they value communication. Men want to be respected, in marriage and the greater society. David Murrow says that men want to be great.

"What does all this mean? If you want to capture the heart of a man, especially a younger man, you have to offer him a shot at greatness. Men will not invest themselves wholeheartedly in any endeavor that does not offer this

65

possibility. The world offers men the possibility of greatness. The world cheers for men. Too often a local church does not. What a tragedy. It's no sin to recognize men for the good they do. It is not about exalting individuals; it's about celebrating what God is doing in people's lives. Ever since Abraham, men have wanted to become great. Is this so bad? What if the church, instead of opposing men in this dream, actively partnered with them? What if the church focused on raising up men of wisdom, character, and strength? What if your church were in the business of turning out great men?"[8]

Men are tired of hearing about the bad news that describes Black manhood. We know all about the prison stats, the drug stats, the fatherlessness stats. Men want to hear good news. They want to hear about the number of men in college, the number of men who stayed with their children, the number of men who stayed in the Lord, the number of men who've started successful businesses.

Wives, never give your husband a tape of your pastor badgering men for their nonattendance in church (or other things). Too few pastors highlight the great deeds done by men in the community. The wise pastor knows that a little stroking of the male ego can go a long way in terms of church involvement and more regular attendance.

So-called "prosperity churches," where the only person in the church prospering is the pastor, are another major problem. How can some wealthy pastors boast about their possessions and high income on the pulpit while their congregation is trying to tithe and make offerings out of social security checks, pension and welfare checks? Who in the church besides the pastor has an airplane, a Bentley, a mansion, and a seven-figure bank account? If the congregation as a whole is prospering, then men will be more inclined to attend. Men want to be great Christians, but if only the pastor is prospering—and boasting besides—men will stay away in droves.

Men want to be great and want to make a difference. Men want their lives to count. They want meaning. They want to make an impact, a contribution. They want to do something important. They want to conquer. They want to be somebody. They want to be significant.

A young man killed a college female. When asked why he did it, he said he wanted to be on television. He wanted to be great. He wanted to be seen and heard. Can you imagine, Satan had such a hold on him that he thought the only way to appear on television was to commit murder? Have we reached such an all-time low that some men feel the only way to be great is to take another person's life?

Often, schools bring me in to motivate students—boys in particular because faculty and staff say they have low self-esteem. I tell them to observe the boys on the playground, in their neighborhoods, in any environment other than the classroom. Boys and young men are highly confident on the basketball court, rapping with friends, and talking to girlfriends. Clearly, there is a distinction between self-esteem and school-esteem. Their problem is being in ninth grade with a third-grade reading level. The effective school will figure out ways to tap into boys' innate strengths and creatively apply them to the classroom.

Black men want to be great financial providers. There's no tremendous difference between Black men and White men in this regard. It is difficult being a man in America, a country that is capitalistic and patriarchal, without capital. In the Young Adult Male Ministries chapter, we will look at the impact that economics has on Black manhood. People can criticize 50 Cent, P Diddy, Snoop, and all the ball players that they want, but these men have become financially great, especially in the eyes of males 12 to 35 years of age.

Sports, rap, and the drug culture have taken over the church in providing young Black males opportunities to be great. For 16-year-old Black males who have dropped out of school, nearly guaranteeing few to no opportunities to matriculate through the economy, the only way to achieve greatness is to sell crack cocaine.

What types of church ministries will empower Black males to be great? Is there room in the church for males other than the pastor to be great?

We need to study why, in the Black community, there is often more than one church on a block. Surely one strong church would be more effective in evangelism, missions, and ministry than four struggling storefronts that are barely able to pay their utility bills. Perhaps the reason why four churches reside on the same block is because three of the pastors didn't feel important when they used to attend the first church.

Position, territory, and power are important to men. These are key factors in the way we become great. How can the pastor maintain his position while sharing power and territory with other men? Surely there's more than enough room in the body of Christ for more than just one strong male leader. This is critical in retaining men, and if the church can find creative, spirit-led ways to resolve this issue, our churches will become stronger. I encourage pastors and church leaders to study Paul's letters to the churches in depth. Like today, church leaders were often in conflict as to how to grow the new church and deal with persecution.

Several books have been written in the past decade that have been critical of the church. I bring this up because men often use the arguments found in these books to justify not going to church. Don't throw the baby out with the bathwater. In Paul's day, criticism was hurled at the church. There will always be criticism. While people have a right to their opinions, consider their agenda and beliefs. Most of these books were written by nonbelievers, people who do not believe that Jesus is Lord, and many are more concerned about exposing the flaws of the pastor than revealing the Good News about the Savior. Truthfully, it wouldn't matter if the pastor improved or not because these writers don't believe that Jesus Christ is the Son of God, and this unbelief holds the clue to understanding their agenda. Some folk just have a problem with our faith and will do everything in their power to come against it.

These writers ignore the great works being done by so many churches while spotlighting ineffective entertainment and containment theologies. What it comes down to is this: they do not want people to accept Jesus as Lord. Don't be misled.

How do we make men great? How can we make the church a breeding ground for male greatness? How does the church compete against the streets, the basketball court, gangs, rappers, and the drug culture? These are the major questions we explore in seminars and retreats, but we won't be able to resolve these issues quickly. It requires serious thought. The male ego is large, fragile, and sensitive. Many schools that do not understand the male ego believe, like the military, that they have to break boys down and then build them back up.

The spirits of our men have been broken, not only by schools but by the larger society. Ralph Ellison in the powerful book *The Invisible Man* describes how many Black men in our racist, capitalistic, patriarchal society feel invisible. What can the church do to make men visible? What can the church do to make Black men feel important? What can the church do to stroke and develop the male ego?

There are churches that have many ministries, 100 or more, and the pastor attempts to head each one. This makes no sense. One way to empower men and make them feel important is for Moses to pass the baton to Joshua just as Elijah passed the baton to Elisha. Pastors must pass the baton to other men and make them feel important. If the pastor's ego does not allow him to share greatness with other men growth and effectiveness is going to be limited because one man cannot be in a hundred different places simultaneously.

More churches should have Man of the Month or Man of the Year awards. Men could be nominated by their families, ministers, and members of the church so that they could be recognized for their good works.

Black men, especially 12 to 35 year olds, believe their greatest need is money. Matthew 6:33 says, "But seek first the kingdom of God and His righteousness, and all these things shall be added to you." When we evangelize in low-income communities and overseas, we must meet the people at their point of need first before sharing the Word of God. It is unfortunate that we can't do what Matthews 6:33 says in every situation. It is difficult to give a starving family the Word of God when they are hungry. If you look at the gospels and the ministry of Jesus Christ, He met them first at their point of need.

For Black men, we need to understand that they believe their greatest need is financial. Those of us who are more mature in the Word know, however, that their greatest need is spiritual. The natural man cannot discern spiritual things. Most men are not aware that their greatest need is spiritual. Let me give you an example. If a man has a personal relationship with Jesus Christ, then he will understand Joshua 1:5: "No man shall be able to stand before you all the days of your life; as I was with Moses, so I will be with you. I will not leave you nor forsake you."

Joshua 1:8 reads, "This Book of the Law shall not depart from your mouth, but you shall meditate in it day and night, that you may observe to do according to all that is written in it. For then *you* will make your way prosperous, and then *you* will have good success" (my emphasis). Unfortunately, many men think it's the White man that's holding them back, but if you fully understand Joshua 1:5, it clearly says *no* man—that includes the White man. If *you* meditate in the Word day and night, no system, including racism, will be able to hold you back.

So, a man who understands Matthew 6:33 ("seek first the Kingdom of God") and Joshua 1:5 could be laid off of his job, but because he has a personal relationship with Jesus Christ and because he understands that God is the source of his power, he will create another job. Good things will happen to him. His confession will line up with the Word of God. That man is being led by the Spirit.

For the majority of men who are being led by their eyes, we will have to provide them with something they can see. When Pastor Winston showed the young men the mall and the economic opportunities, then and only then were they willing to listen to what he had to say about the Word of God.

One difference between men and women is that men like to debate, to challenge each other, to discuss the issues. One of the things I love about the barbershop is that I'm not "Dr. Kunjufu" when I'm getting my hair cut. I'm just another brother with an opinion, and everybody's opinion matters. Brothers will come out of left field with their analysis and everybody's entitled to their opinion. Every brother feels that their opinion is correct. They will challenge you, argue, discuss, and debate. Men just like that give and take. Unfortunately, they don't get that opportunity in church.

Everyone has a testimony, and many men would love to share theirs, but they have never been given the opportunity. The church should be a place where people can share their testimonies about what the Lord has done for them. Young men and men who have not made the most important decision of their lives need to hear men reveal their faith.

I enjoy it when men share their testimonies in retreats and seminars. Not only is it therapeutic for the man giving the testimony, but it increases the faith of all those who hear it.

What do men need? Men need to defend themselves against Satan's attacks. Satan knows that men are visual, and this is one of our greatest weaknesses. The natural man (and his eyes) cannot discern the things of the Spirit.

Pornography was designed by Satan for men's eyes, and it is running rampant. Pornography (via print, video, online, cable) is a multi-billion dollar industry—and it is destroying families. Men are making pornography their god, their mistress. Men will tell their wives that they can't have sex unless they watch a video first. Can you imagine how she feels? Pornography addicts spend hours upon hours on the Internet, watching videos, and looking at pictures in magazines. If you asked these addicts if they're having an adulterous affair, they would say no, because they're not involved in the sexual act. Their wives might feel differently.

I will never forget the story that was given to me by the manager of a hotel that was hosting a ministerial conference. I was trying to witness to this man about the goodness of the Lord, but he quickly said, "I don't want to hear anything about your God." The hotel has more than 1,000 rooms, and all were filled with ministers. The manager had documented and showed me that whenever this convention comes to town, these ministers continually break records of renting pornographic movies to view in their rooms. Again, the hotel manager said, "I don't want anything to do with your God."

Now you tell me what my response to this man should have been? He had documented proof of a great sin that had been committed by the leaders of the church.

For most men, a desire for sex is as fundamental as a desire for food, and not only does something die inside a married man when this desire isn't met, something can also be perverted for lack of pure fulfillment.

Attempting to ward off or at least cope with the hurt, Christian men try to joke about it. Here are just some of the names I've heard to describe unsatisfying sex: Check-her-pulse sex, did-I-detect life? sex, refund sex, mercy sex, pity sex, I'm- tired-so-hurry-up sex, 50%-off sex, 9-1-1 sex, undertaker sex, wouldn't-pass-lie-detector sex, jewelry sex, new-car sex, and bigger-home sex. *What we really want and need is There's-No-One-Like-You sex.*

Here's a somewhat famous letter, circulated among disgruntled husbands, that attempts to salve their pain with humor:

To My Loving Wife:

During the past year I have tried to make love to you 365 times. I have succeeded only thirty-six times, an average of once every ten days. The following is a list of the reasons why I did not succeed more often: it was too late, too early, too hot, or too cold. It would awaken the children, the company in the next room, or the neighbors whose windows were open. You were too full, or you had a headache, a backache, a toothache, or the giggles. You pretended to be asleep or were not in the mood. You had on your mudpack. You watched the late TV show; I watched the late TV show; the baby was crying.

During the times I did succeed, the activity was not entirely satisfactory for a variety of reasons. On six occasions you chewed gum the whole time; every so often you watched TV the whole time. Frequently you told me to hurry up and get it over with. A few times I tried to awaken you to tell you we were through; and one time I was afraid I had hurt you, for I felt you move.

Honey, it's no wonder I drink too much.

                                        Your Loving Husband

The Bible teaches that God looked at man and said he needed help. Out of his side, not his back, he drew woman. Satan observed something when this happened. The man was so excited when he saw her. Men are visual. When he set his eyes on her, he was so excited. He looked at her, but all he could say was "wowowowowowowo—woman!"

Satan thought, "This is how I will bring him down." The Bible reminds us in Proverbs 7:21–27:

"With her enticing speech she caused him to yield, With her flattering lips she seduced him.

Immediately he went after her, as an ox goes to the slaughter, Or as a fool to the correction of the stocks,

Till an arrow struck his liver. As a bird hastens to the snare, He did not know it *would cost* his life.

Now therefore, listen to me, *my* children; Pay attention to the words of my mouth:

Do not let your heart turn aside to her ways, Do not stray into her paths;

For she has cast down many wounded, And all who were slain by her were strong *men.*

Her house *is* the way to hell, Descending to the chambers of death."

How many men have we lost because of lust, adultery, pornography, and fornication? The Bible reminds us that "all who were slain by her were strong men."

Satan got three of our best in the Bible: one who had a heart like God, David; one who was considered the smartest in the Bible, Solomon; and one who was considered the strongest, Sampson. How foolish we are to think that if Satan got David, Solomon, and Sampson that he would not get us. What makes the problem even more acute in the Black community is that with the shortage of Black men, Black women are making it easier for Black men to take advantage of them. Brother, do you think you're all that, or are you in demand because the ratio is 3:1?

What Men Need

And don't think a woman can become choosy and want an employed, educated, saved Black man. Her choices become far and few in between. On some college campuses, the ratio is ten females to one male. I've been to some churches where it's a near 5:1 ratio.

It's true that Satan got David, Solomon, and Sampson, but there is a man in the Bible who knew what to do, who did not let pornography and adultery take him out. I'm not talking about Jesus—I'm talking about Joseph.

What do men need? Men need to study Joseph. They need to study Genesis 39:7–12:

"And it came to pass after these things that his master's wife cast longing eyes on Joseph, and she said, 'Lie with me.'

"But he refused and said to his master's wife, 'Look, my master does not know what *is* with me in the house, and he has committed all that he has to my hand.

There is no one greater in this house than I, nor has he kept back anything from me but you, because you *are* his wife. How then can I do this great wickedness, and sin against God?'

"So it was, as she spoke to Joseph day by day, that he did not heed her, to lie with her *or* to be with her.

"But it happened about this time, when Joseph went into the house to do his work, and none of the men of the house *was* inside, that she caught him by his garment, saying, 'Lie with me.' But he left his garment in her hand, *and fled and ran outside*" (my emphasis).

What do strong men do in certain situations? They run. Sometimes you can't stay. Sometimes you can't negotiate. Sometimes you just have to run.

We can learn a lot from Joseph. I can assure you, my brothers, Satan knows your weakness. It is a naive man who does not study his own weaknesses. As a tennis player, I always play to my opponent's weaknesses. Once I know his weaknesses, then I know where to send the ball, and as often as possible.

It's the same thing with Satan. He knows our weaknesses. If he knows you're visual, if he knows you like women, if he knows you like pretty women, then regardless of your position, marital, financial, and educational status, Satan knows he can bring you down.

It has taken me a long time to get to the heart of this book, but now that our foundation has been laid, we can take a look at male ministries that are needed in the church.

CHAPTER 7:
MALE MINISTRIES

What are the basic needs of men? When we know men's needs, then we can begin to develop effective ministries. Pastors, consider developing a questionnaire for men to complete that would help you develop or improve your male ministries.

Listed below are various issues that men deal with on a daily basis. Please rank your top five.

- Spiritual growth
- Bible knowledge
- Evangelism
- Missions
- Mentoring
- Marriage
- Fathering
- Friendships
- Sexuality
- Physical fitness
- Life purpose
- Jobs/career
- Finances
- Time/priorities
- Male passivity
- Emotional balance
- Domestic violence
- Pornography
- Substance abuse
- Crime
- Prison
- AIDS
- Other

Good leaders are good listeners and good followers. They are attentive to the needs of men. If the men emphasize certain issues over others, then the leadership should acquiesce and consider the needs of its membership. Also, have men in the larger community complete the questionnaire. I love to speak at church events where the larger community has been invited. Unchurched men often attend in good numbers.

Based on my observations of churches over the past 30 years, the following are some of the more traditional ministries that men participate in:

- Usher
- Trustee
- Deacon
- Choir
- Building maintenance
- Greeter
- Music
- Broadcast
- Sunday school teacher
- Kitchen
- Men's fellowship
- Cub/boy scouts
- Rites of passage
- Security
- Mentoring
- Credit union
- Medical
- Drama
- Education/scholarship
- Prison
- Drug-free ministry
- Sports/recreation
- Singles
- Couples
- Evangelism
- Missions

Male Ministries

If we're going to be effective, we must begin to think out of the box. If we keep doing what we've been doing and expect a different outcome, this borders on insanity. Compare and contrast responses to the questionnaire (especially in the "Other" category) to the male ministries that already exist in your church, and you will begin to see some interesting issues take shape.

Ask yourself if your ministries are truly meeting the needs of men. Are they too traditional? Who do they really benefit?

Next, look at how you're managing your ministries. The five major problems with ministries, specifically men's ministries, are as follows:

1. Lack of prayer.
2. Led by one.
3. Based only on activities and events.
4. Based on random activities.
5. Based on methods.

Lack of prayer. Your ministry will only move forward on its knees. Successful ministries are praying ministries. Appoint two or three men as prayer warriors of the ministry, and make sure they know how to pray and do spiritual warfare. Many people do not know how to pray. For instance, when people pray over their food, the prayer might not even address the eating of the meal.

Prayers need to be specific. They need to include the name of Jesus. They need to include the blood. We need warriors who will pray with authority, which means they know how to bind and loose (Matthew 18:18). Jesus is clear: "Whatever you bind on earth will be bound in heaven, and whatever you loose on earth will be loosed in heaven."

We need to align our prayers with our words. You will dilute your prayer for healing or whatever you're praying for if you conclude with "if it's Your will." Pray His will by praying His Word. If His Word says He can heal all diseases, that's what you need to pray.

Led by one. What would happen to the ministry if the leader was no longer present? Effective ministries are based on a team approach rather than individuals running everything. Think of coaches and their players. The leader of the ministry, the coach, has the vision and has done great things. Coaches, however, do not play the game. They empower players to execute the plan. I love coaches who, when the team has won, defer credit to the players. One of the major reasons why there are so many problems in ministries is because the leaders have burned out and they didn't train captains and lieutenants to carry on.

Based only on activities and events. You can burn out your men by having events after events after events. By being so event-focused, there are few opportunities to form relationships because everyone is working nonstop.

A husband and wife were discussing their various ministries. When the wife shared all of what her women's ministry was doing, the husband said, "What's the date of the event? Who are the speakers? Where's it going to be?" Purely logistical issues. The wife reminded her husband, "We're talking about women's ministry. We're not like you. We can come together just to be with each other. There doesn't have to be a topic. We don't have to have a speaker. We don't have to have goals and objectives." There needs to be a balance between activities and relationships.

Based on random activities. There should be some relationship between big events and ministering to the needs of men. Some churches measure success by the celebrity of the speaker, the swank hotel where the event was held, and the number of tickets that were sold. But the poignant question is, where do we go from here? Is there a relationship between this event and Monday night's Bible study? What was the purpose of the event? What were its goals and objectives? Were the purpose, goals, and objectives lined up with the ministry's mission statement?

That may be the problem. Is there a mission statement? What is the vision of the ministry?

Based on methods. What works for one church may not work for your church. You can get ideas from other ministries, but when it comes right down to it, you've got to do your homework. Start with developing the questionnaire and having men complete it.

I have always been interested in geographical differences in Black America. The Black family is not monolithic. Twenty-five percent of African American families earn more than $75,000; 33 percent live below the poverty line. There's a widening gap between the Black haves and have nots.

A church in a community of Black haves has different needs from a church in a community of Black have nots. Living in Harlem is tremendously different from living in Hope, Arkansas. There's a difference between living in Boston, Massachusetts, in the winter and living in Miami, Florida, during hurricane season. There's a difference between living in Atlanta, an intellectual mecca with six Black colleges, vs. living in Minnesota where African Americans are less than 5 percent of the population.

Ministries must address the needs of their individual church and not simply duplicate what other ministries are doing across the country.

The book, *Effective Men's Ministry,* edited by Phil Downer, lists the following warnings:

1. Don't start without pastoral support.
2. Don't start without prayer.
3. Don't start without key people.
4. Don't start without preparation.
5. Don't try to do too much too fast.
6. Don't create events for everyone.
7. Don't limit events by age.
8. Don't be boring and disorganized.
9. Don't start without input from a variety of other men.
10. Don't make decisions without a proper plan

11. Don't try to develop a plan without prayer.
12. Don't do the same things at every event.
13. Don't neglect small groups.
14. Don't neglect the discipleship.
15. Don't reinvent the wheel.
16. Don't be a one-man show.
17. Don't think too small or too big.
18. Don't wait for next year. Begin now.

David Murrow offers the following advice:

"Always stress the purpose when announcing events. Here's a bulletin announcement that misses the mark: 'The annual men's retreat will be held June 8 at Lake Arrowhead. Our speaker will be John Armstrong. Cost is $65. To sign up, call Steve Stanley.' What's wrong with this announcement? It never states the purpose of the retreat. If you're asking a guy to give up two days of his life, you need to clearly state what's in it for him."

Another observation that he makes:

"Tony went to men's small group in his church once. First the men sat in a circle and sang praise songs for about ten minutes. Tony was asked to introduce himself and share about his life. Next he was paired with a stranger and asked to share one of his deepest fears. Then everyone was asked to share a prayer need or praise report. The men read from the Bible, taking turns around the circle. Finally the men stood in the circle and held hands for what seemed like hours while one by one they bared their souls to God. One man was quietly weeping. The guy next to Tony prayed for ten minutes straight and his palms were sweaty. Once the meeting was over Tony didn't stay for cookies. He hasn't been back."[9]

Male Ministries

Can you imagine a 12-to 35-year-old street brother in a circle primarily filled with elderly men? Why don't Black men go to church? Because they've been, and Tony has not been back.

If we're going to develop effective male ministries, we need to draw upon the resources of all groups. The ministry cannot be dominated by elderly men. It needs to be equally balanced by age group. It also needs to be equally balanced based on income and education. It needs to be balanced based on geography. Brothers from one side of town may have different interests from those on the other side of town.

Disciples and Workers

Howard Hendricks from Dallas Theological Seminary sees two kinds of people in the church: the pillars and the caterpillars. The pillars uphold the church with their prayers, work, and donations. They build the Kingdom of God by the sweat of their brows. The caterpillars crawl in on Sunday morning, sing a few songs, listen to a sermon, and crawl out again, not to be seen for a week if not longer.

If your church is typical, most of the pillars are female. Women are more likely than men to devote themselves to Christianity beyond simple church attendance. Researcher George Barna found that women are:

"100 percent more likely to be involved in discipleship.

57 percent more likely to participate in adult Sunday school.

56 percent more likely to hold a leadership position at a church.

54 percent more likely to participate in a small group.

46 percent more likely to disciple others.

39 percent more likely to have a devotional time or a quiet time.

33 percent more likely to volunteer for church.
29 percent more likely to read the Bible.
29 percent more likely to attend church.
29 percent more likely to share faith with others.
23 percent more likely to donate to a church.
16 percent more likely to pray."[10]

We must change this paradigm. Not only do we need to increase the number of men in church, but somehow we must transform male caterpillars to pillars.

I am reminded of Jesus' charge in the Bible, and it was not to go make workers. It was to go and make disciples. Pillars are disciples and disciples are pillars. When you balance your ministries' focuses to include both events and relationships, then the need for workers will give way to the development of discipleship among men.

But what do churches do? To keep the production of events going throughout the year, hundreds of workers are put into service. One event is barely over before the next big one is being planned. The men burn out, and they need rest before the next event. Unfortunately, in the interim, there's little done to develop relationships and disciples.

There's a major distinction between a disciple and a worker. A worker is viewed like an object—a hammer, screwdriver, tool, something to be used and consumed, and when unable to function you simply throw it out and secure another tool, another worker. Is that how we treat our men? Or do we treat them as disciples, humans, people with frailties, people who have needs, desires, and aspirations?

One of the most powerful scenes in the Bible is when Peter betrayed Jesus three times, and yet said to His face that he would never deny Him. When Jesus rose, one of the first things He said was, "Go and tell Peter." It was obvious that Jesus knew that despite the betrayal, there was much more to Peter than fear.

Male Ministries

God knew us in the womb. He knows the end from the beginning. Jesus knew how powerful Peter was going to be in the future as a preacher and disciple. He saw him as far more than just a worker.

Church leadership needs to see their men not just as workers and tools, but as disciples, as humans who need relationship.

There is a rule, unfortunately, in most churches that reinforces the pillar and the caterpillar dichotomy. Some of you've heard of it as the 5 to 95 Rule, the 10 to 90 Rule, and the 20 to 80 Rule. The theory says that 5 percent of the people do 95 percent of the work. Ten percent of the people do 90 percent of the work. Twenty percent of the people do 80 percent of the work. The paradigm needs to change. The 5, 10, and 20 percent of workers are burning out.

I can't tell you the number of rites of passage programs I have worked with in churches, only to find out several years later that the program is in the doldrums because the workers burned out.

It's like a football game where you have a stadium of 100,000 people, mostly men, and millions more are watching on television, observing 22 men exercise. That's the way I see ministry going on in churches. You have hundreds of people watching a few pillars do the majority of the work.

Not only do men have a desire to be great and respected, they need challenges, goals. They also need a beginning and an end. If your neighborhood is filled with liquor stores and crack houses, then you must develop ministries to address those concerns. If you have highway construction in your neighborhood with no Black workers being used, then we need a ministry that will address this problem.

Men like clear beginnings and clear endings. They don't want programs and projects to go on and on or else they will get easily bored. However, we have to go beyond our comfort zone on this one. Because of the chronic epidemic of fatherlessness in our community, our boys need long-term mentoring. When you commit to mentor a boy or young adult male, there may be no ending. For men with short attention spans, they seem unable to focus on a particular issue longer than six months, maybe a couple of years. Programs that require more than a three-year commitment will unfortunately see men's involvement taper off.

Here's where the issue of discipleship comes in. Workers will quit, but disciples will stay for the long term.

Reinvigorate your ministry and attract new blood so the "this is the way we've always done it" philosophy does not have a chance to take root. Your ministry will quickly die if the younger men are not given a chance to develop and implement their fresh, new ideas.

Leaders of successful ministries internalize the role of servant. Steve Sonderman in the *How to Build a Life Changing Men's Ministries* says,

"I have found it exceedingly easy to find men who want to be involved in ministry as long as they start at the top and don't have to do the ordinary, dirty jobs. They want to be up front teaching or around the table, making decisions, not in the back making coffee, setting up chairs. Sometimes I get the impression some men feel they are above certain tasks. They import their marketplace position, power, and philosophy and believe it will work in the church. It doesn't and it shouldn't. To serve another man is to invest in his life. It's interesting when you study Jesus' life to note that He too never asked the disciples to do anything that He wasn't willing to do Himself. He asked them to pray, and He prayed. He asked them to serve, and He washed their feet. He asked them to love one another, and He died on the Cross for them."[11]

Yes, we want to be great, but we must balance the desire for greatness with the commitment to serve. That means that sometimes you may have to work behind the scenes. The point is to get the job done. As Martin Luther King taught us before he died, to be a good leader is to be a good servant.

Male Ministries

Outreach

What percentage of your ministries takes place outside of your church?

Many churches feel they have the answers, and the only way for you to receive their wisdom is for you to come inside of the church. I call it "home field advantage." What percentage of Jesus' ministry was inside the synagogue? When He healed people, was that inside or outside the sanctuary? When He fed people, was that inside or outside the synagogue? When He called Lazarus from the dead, was He inside or outside the sanctuary? If you look at the ministry of Jesus, He did not rely on the church. He did not need home field advantage.

We have become too comfortable inside of our churches. We need to take our ministries, as much as possible, to the streets like Jesus did. Later, we will review the successful efforts of one church to eradicate liquor stores from the neighborhood. The church had to go out into the streets to accomplish this goal. To eliminate drug dealers from the neighborhood, you must leave your sanctuary and go out into the streets.

I love the work of Vineyard Community Church in Cincinnati. They repair houses, perform car repairs, and improve the overall quality of life in the community. The men love it and the community benefits from the ministry. Vineyard is not dependent on sermons to teach the Word of God. When men witness other men doing this kind of work, physical labor, not only is it something they can do, they also know it's being done for the Lord.

It's one thing to hear a sermon. It's another thing to see a sermon.

I have always been impressed with the boldness of the Jehovah Witnesses and the Nation of Islam as they walk the streets in our neighborhoods. They realize the importance of ministry outside of the sanctuary. Although there are more Christians than Muslims and Jehovah Witnesses, you seldom see Christians regularly evangelizing on the street. This is unfortunate and adds to the impression among men that the church is out of touch.

African American male inmates will tell you they see more Muslims, Jehovah Witnesses, and White Christians than they see African Americans, and specifically African American male Christians, who are willing to leave their church and go into the prisons to minister.

Powerhouse Christian Center in Katy, Texas, is a different kind of church. It is built on the principles of spiritual fathering. Powerhouse is growing rapidly and enjoys astronomical male retention, giving, and participation. Church officials report the following:

- Nearly 50 percent of first time visitors become regular attendees.
- 60 to 65 percent of new converts stay in church.
- On average, 60 percent of those who attend Sunday morning services attend home groups.
- 60 percent of the members tithe.
- Half the multi-ethnic congregation is male. Even more remarkable, the men seem to enjoy being there.

During the worship service, things move along and no element of the worship service takes more than ten minutes. There's almost always live drama or a video produced in the church's onsite studio. The sermon is brief and packed with masculine imagery and illustrations.

The hidden strength of the church is its structure. There are no committees. Instead, the pastor serves as a spiritual father to a dozen men. Each of these men fathers 12 men, who in turn father up to 12 men, and the list goes on. The pastor meets with his sons weekly for prayer and instruction. They hold each other accountable. Powerhouse calls this "male mentoring."

This is just one example of many that we will look at in this book. In the next chapter, we will look at one of my major concerns, and that's developing strong teenage male ministries.

CHAPTER 8:
TEENAGE MALE MINISTRIES

In the powerful book *The Hip Hop Church* authors Smith and Jackson share the following:

In some ways youth can feel like second-class citizens, in the church, sitting in the back of the church while the adults "get their praise on." When youth are recognized, it is because they are serving in the youth choir, youth usher board or youth council—merely mimicking adults and their behavior in the church. I'm not saying that this setup in and of itself is bad, but it can keep youth from feeling that they have their own space and platform for expression within the church, coming from their own generational experience.

The complication with the African American congregation in relation to hip-hop is that the church is void of solid youth ministry programming. Typically, there is one youth day a year, presided over by Reverend Johnson, who is so far removed from youth that his message is irrelevant. The junior ushers, junior preachers, junior elders and junior everything for this one day make up the entire youth program. There are no empowering ministry components that would bring holistic deliverance to the lives of students. Hip-hop brings juice to the life of a student—juice right now—empowerment and the sense that they are important.

But to start a hip-hop church is no easy thing. Too many times in Christendom we are too quick to grab hold of the next gimmick and run with it until the leader realizes the people are not excited about this anymore. Look in your church basement, or any church basement, in the storage area, and you will find books, manuals, products, puppet curtains, videos, more manuals on whatever was the trend or fad awhile back—and now that the organizer has moved on or the gimmick proved too hard to pull off, all the stuff has just been put away. Another indication is the famous statement "God led us *for a season* to host a hip-hop church." Tell the truth! The truth is you didn't know what the heck you were getting into![12]

My love and my heart go out to this age group. This is the group that's least represented in church and causing the greatest havoc in our community. I call this group "young warriors." Many of them have a warrior spirit. Let me briefly describe the warrior spirit.

- Like hunters, they prefer being outside.
- They have no fear.
- They don't play by the odds.
- They want to claim and protect turf.
- They often have a chip on their shoulder.
- They react first and think second.
- They're sensitive about someone violating their manhood.
- They're stronger physically than mentally or spiritually.

The best place for warriors is in church, but is the church ready for warriors? Is the church designed to provide programs for warriors?

What is the church doing to equip a 16-year-old male who is being bullied on his way to school? Is the church providing any direction, any guidelines or advice for this young man?

Rap has a tremendous impact on our youth.

• In 1950, the greatest influences on youth were home, school, church, peer pressure, and television.

• In 2006, the greatest influences are rap, television, peer pressure, home, and school. Rap has now moved to the number one position. Is 50 Cent raising our children?

• Not all rap is negative, but youth say that adults put all rap in the same genre.

• In my book *Hip Hop: A Street Curriculum,* I mentioned four companies that are controlling the minds of our youth: Universal, EMI, Warner, and Sony/BMG.

• There are more than 5,000 rap songs to play on any given day, yet radio stations and television music programs choose the 40 most vile gangster rap songs and play them over and over again.

Authors and pastors Efrem Smith and Phil Jackson make the following observation:

Are the church and hip hop on a *collision* course, as both battle for the hearts and minds of young unchurched people within hip hop culture? This position sees hip hop as rap music that is corrupting our youth. The two are thus in a battle for young people—and it seems that rap music is winning.

Is it *compromising* the Good News, the gospel of Jesus Christ, for the church to use hip hop elements as tools for evangelism and discipleship? When gospel artists such as Kirk Franklin and Hezekiah Walker use the work of mainstream hip hop artists such as R. Kelly or Sean "Puffy" Combs, are they compromising their mission?

As pastors, we lead churches that use elements of hip hop not only in the worship experience but also as outreach tools. The *coexistence* position sees hip hop not just as music but as a culture, a milieu in which we are living and growing up. Hip hop culture can be used as a vehicle to express the Good News in a relevant way to the current generation.[13]

Holy Hip Hop
(Some Christian Rappers)

D.C. Talk
Altar Nation
Verbal Witness
Messenger 777
Charmel
Kirk Franklin
I D O L King
Freedom of Soul
Soldiers for Christ
Transformation Crusade
D.O.C. (Disciples of Christ)
Holy Hip Hop Taking the Gospel to the Streets (Grammy nomination featuring a variety of Christian hip hop artists)
Fred Lynch has created a hip hop version of the Gospel of John, The Epic (www.gettheepic.com)

Some Hip Hop Ministries

House Covenant Church, Chicago
Sanctuary Covenant Church, Minneapolis
Crossover Church, Tampa
New Life Fellowship, New York
Sound Changers, Carey, North Carolina

Teenage Male Ministries

Hip Hop Haven

Haughville City Hill Church outside of Indianapolis is in a run down, crime infested neighborhood. They have created a Friday night session called "Hip Hop Haven." It provides a safe environment for nearly 400 youth ages 8 to 15. They give away food and drink and offer kids the use of ten televisions equipped with a variety of nonviolent video games.

Pastor Rodger Holloway, a former radio disc jockey, has equipped his church with a $50,000 sound system. From 7:00 pm to 10:00 pm, strobe lights and a fog machine are turned on. Christian Hip Hop music is played. Holloway does not allow any dirty dancing. Often, he will bring in a guest speaker, celebrity, inspirational speaker, or Bible preacher.

What I like about Hip Hop Haven is that the young people are off the streets Friday night, one of the most dangerous nights of the week for youth. Churches wanting to adapt this program to their youth ministry could open their doors on Saturday nights so that youth can enjoy a safe haven in the house of the Lord. Hip Hop Haven can include gospel and positive rap, choir rehearsal, positive videos, roller skating, card games, nonviolent video games, pizza parties—whatever you think is appropriate for youth.

In addition, the youth could sleep over in sleeping bags or on cots. Early Sunday morning they could wake up, receive breakfast, and then go into the house of the Lord for worship. A Hip Hop Haven guarantees that our youth are not involved in any violent or criminal activity. Children are taught values and given direction that right now are being primarily provided by gangs and gangster rappers.

I have shared the concept of Hip Hop Haven with churches, and many have tried it. They brought in 300 youth. The ratio was 10 to 1 between youth and mentors. The problem is that most of the volunteer mentors were female although half the youth were male. So you have mostly adult women giving direction to males. Many pastors have shied away. Hip

Hop Haven has done a great job in Indianapolis, and I believe it can be implemented nationwide, including your church. But men must make a commitment and stick with it.

To implement Hip Hop Haven in your church, you will need the following:

- An adequate sound system
- Positive rap CDs (provided by youth)
- A large television screen
- Positive videos (preferably gospel)
- Evening meal or snacks and breakfast (for Sunday morning)
- A 10:1 ratio of adult male mentors to youth
- Space for dancing or roller skating (optional)
- Nonviolent video games
- Constructive card games.

As you can see, Hip Hop Haven doesn't require much capital. It just requires a vision to begin to give direction to our youth.

One of the unfortunate realities negatively impacting teen life are gangs. Why do young people join gangs?

1. Money. Many youth join gangs to make fast money. Financially disadvantaged young people look for ways to buy expensive starter jackets, tennis shoes, and electronic equipment. They'd rather participate in one drug deal and make enough money to buy something that would take a full month to earn by working at a fast food restaurant.

2. Power. Gangs promise power to youth who feel powerless over their lives. Although the power is a false sense of security, they have no other healthy sources for support.

3. Identity. Many youth are desperately searching for a place to belong. Gangs accept youth who don't feel loved or accepted by parents, adults, or school. Gang identity also offers members guidelines on how to act and dress.

4. Protection. Many youth feel forced to join a gang for protection from other gangs, especially in the inner city. The gang provides a false sense of protection from the law.

5. Fun. Gangs provide activities and a social life. Many youth enjoy living on the edge and participating in dangerous activities. What first appears to be fun usually has serious consequences.

6. Intimidation. Many youth join gangs because of fear, threats, and intimidation from other gang members or bullies. Young people may want to join a gang to appear tough or more acceptable.

7. Shock. If young people aren't getting positive attention from parents, joining a gang certainly provides lots of negative attention. Youth who are angry at a parent may join a gang to shock or to be defiant.

8. Romance. Many young people don't know what gangs are really about and have a misguided sense of romance about them. They might think they can join the gang for fun and get out whenever they wish. They might also believe that joining a gang will not involve them in violence and criminal activity.

9. Family Involvement. Family members in gangs often recruit other family members. Young people who grow up with a parent involved in a gang are at extreme risk of joining a gang. Gang involvement becomes a way of life for some families.

10. Low Self-Esteem. Youth who don't feel good about themselves are more vulnerable, and they will seek out ways to feel accepted. If healthy options aren't available, they may look to gangs for support.

11. Academic Problems. Young people who are not finding success at school may see no hope or future for themselves in education. Many don't believe they could ever get a good job or go to college, so they look for other alternatives.

We need churches and Christian leaders to address these 11 reasons why young people join gangs. We need ministries that will address each of these issues if we are serious about reclaiming our youth.

Let me share with you a horror story that occurred in Boston.

A wake service was held in a small Black Baptist church. The funeral service of a 20-year-old Dorchester man shot to death at a party Saturday night ended abruptly in pandemonium when a group of youth entered the church and chased down one of the mourners, stabbing him nine times. A panic ensued inside Morningstar Church as more than 300 people who had gathered for the service ran for cover. Shots reportedly were fired both inside and outside the church.

This has to be the turning point for this community, said the Rev. Eugene Rivers of the Azusa Christian Community Church in north Dorchester. He was concerned with a generation of Black males who are plagued by violence. **If the church does not get into the street to recapture an entire generation of young Black men, the street will come violently into the church.**

The church's failure to respond to the plight of the Black male in the underclass is responsible for this tragedy. The church has avoided this and now it has been brought home with brutal clarity (emphasis mine).

Can you imagine the church, an institution that is considered sacred, desecrated by young Black males who are least represented in church? There is strong resentment between these young Black males, these warriors, and elderly Black men that have the church on lock down.

Teenage Male Ministries

One Church, One School

Bishop Henry Williamson founded One Church, One School. The vision is that—

"Every school in America will be in partnership with one or more neighboring churches to improve the academic achievement, social behavior, and personal development of our children and our youth. Our mission—one church, one school—brings together churches and schools in partnerships that teach children to value life and learning. This national network of church-school partnerships also acts as a catalyst to build bridges between other community-based organizations, social service agencies, business enterprises, and other schools.

"The key principal: it takes a whole village to raise a child. One Church, One School utilizes the 'P Principal' of total involvement to provide human and fiscal resources to support a nurturing school and community environment for student development. Pastors, parishioners, principals, parents, pupils, politicians, and philanthropists connect the village to the school and the child."

It is estimated that there are 85,000 churches in Black America. There are only 20,000 schools in Black America. We literally could have four churches for every school. Some schools have no Black adult males in the building. If a Black male does work at a school, chances are he's a custodian first, security guard second, PE teacher third, administrator fourth, and classroom teacher fifth. There are Black boys who have never seen a Black man read a book, write a letter, or operate a computer. Can you imagine how a school would prosper if it were adopted by at least one church that would provide prayer, resources, mentors, equipment, and whatever else is needed?

We need to "call those things which do not exist as though they did" (Romans 4:17), and then watch God work miracles through us and for schools!

One example of a church that did that is pastored by my good friend Frank Reid in Baltimore, Maryland—Bethel A.M.E. Church. Not only do they practice One Church, One School, but they have a ministry called Project Raise. This ministry mentors teenagers from local schools.

After a small riot erupted at Booker T. Washington Junior High School, Bethel began a direct partnership with the school. To prevent a recurrence, Pastor Reid summoned 150 men. They lined the street in front of the school and remained watchful for arsonists, gangs, and visiting troublemakers. At the request of the principal, the men recently returned to supervise the children in the morning and afternoon. The pupils' tranquility prompted one teacher to comment that "they were acting like children again."

Just visualize what Bethel A.M.E. Church had to do to regain order. The gangs thought they had taken over the school. The church, not the Nation of Islam, not the Fruit of Islam, but Christian men, One Church, One School, Project Raise surrounded the school without guns or knives. They were just strong Black men with the blood of Jesus over their lives. Angels on assignment. Hedge of protection around them. Can you imagine nervous students being released from school at the end of the day, worried about making it home in one piece, and then, to their relief, seeing strong Black men surrounding the school and providing protection for *them*? How special and safe they must have felt!

When bullies and gang members see men standing up, they step back. The reason why bullies and gangs feel so confident in our community is because it appears there are only children, women, and elders. But when men step up, bullies and gang members step back.

It is my prayer that every school will become part of One Church, One School. Please visit the website, www.onechurchoneschool.org, and register your church. Learn more about what is needed to become a part of this significant organization. Contact your local school. Talk to your principal. Find out what your school needs. Contact Bethel A.M.E. Church in Baltimore and talk to Frank Reid to learn more about Project Raise. Consider taking your church members to Bethel to learn more about this tremendous program that can provide direction and protection for our youth.

Rites of Passage and Mentoring Programs

I believe the war for the minds of our youth will be between rites of passage programs and gangs. There is a distinction between rites of passage and mentoring programs. In a mentoring program you can have 30 youth and 30 mentors. The mentors could have different values. Some could be gay, some could be straight; some Africentric, some Eurocentric; some illiterate, some college educated. Depending upon your mentor, you could have a totally different experience from other youth in the program. I'm not against mentoring programs, but I am concerned about the tremendous variance that takes place because each mentor is literally allowed to do his own thing.

I'm much more in favor of rites of passage. In rites of passage programs, youth are divided based on gender and age. There is a curriculum that is designed for them to achieve. When they master the curriculum, they can then move from one stage to another stage. Many rites of passage programs use our curriculum SETCLAE. They also use our *Hip Hop Street* curriculum and our textbook, *Lessons from History.* The manuals that we recommend for boys are *Coming of Age* by Paul Hill, *African-centered Rites of Passage* by Lathardus Goggins II, and the manual *Young Lions.* All are available through African American Images (see page 171).

Let me briefly describe how the rites of passage program should be constructed.

1. Organize a group of Black men willing to participate in the program.

2. Develop study sessions with this group, discussing Black history and male development.

3. Identify a facility and decide the frequency and the length of the meetings with the young brothers.

4. The program should provide skill development, Black history, male socialization, recreation, and a mentor.

5. Recommended frequency of meetings is weekly, with one week each allocated to a field trip, the study of Black history, the development of skills, and rites of passage.

6. Field trips should include prison, a drug abuse center, a teenage pregnancy center, a public hospital emergency room on Saturday evening, and a visit to the stock market and local businesses.

7. The nine minimal national standards that all programs should include are spirituality, African history, economics, politics, career development, community involvement, physical development, family responsibility, and values, which include the nguzo saba and maat.

The church is the ideal institution to build rites of passage programs. The following are some questions to consider:

Does your church have a rites of passage program? Is it active?

Did your church have a rites of passage program that died because of coordinator burnout and event fatigue?

What needs to be done to stimulate and reinvigorate your rites of passage program?

Is your rites of passage program open to the larger community, or is it confined to church members?

Basketball Ministry

One of the components of rites of passage is physical development. Earlier I mentioned a run-in I had with a former church member who did not feel that physical development was important. When Jesus saw money changers in His sanctuary, He didn't run to His disciples. He didn't pray or read scripture. He turned those tables over Himself.

I love visiting churches with recreation centers and physical development rooms with weights and training equipment. Our young people need a safe place where they can go to not only learn the word of God, but to develop themselves physically. The Bible says that our body is God's temple and that we reflect God in our body. It is extremely important that our young people, especially young males, feel confident that if someone is messing with them, they have the physical strength to defend themselves. I encourage every church to provide not only weight training and physical development, but to provide their children, especially males, with martial arts training.

If you ask youth what they want to be when they grow up, many will say they want to go pro in the NBA. Our youth literally have eliminated all sports except for basketball. It is no accident that 86 percent of the NBA is African American, but only 1 percent of the engineers, doctors, and dentists are African American.

Many churches have created men's basketball ministries. I want to acknowledge the great work that's been done in the St. Petersburg/Tampa area as part of the faith-based program called the Shepherds Men's Basketball Ministry. It has attracted more than 400 youth and 21 churches participate in the ministry. There is no age limit, but church attendance is required. The motto is "no church, no play." Players pray before and after games. That's one of the reasons why the coordinators said they don't receive grants. They said, "We can't negotiate prayer." Prayer is the cornerstone of this ministry.

The cities have found that one of the best ways to reduce crime in the neighborhood is with midnight basketball. Can't the church do that as well? Churches will always do it better than the government. In addition to basketball, the Shepherds

Men's Basketball Ministry provides mentoring, prayer, values, direction, and keeps our young people off the streets.

The beautiful thing about a Christian basketball ministry is that many of our youth give their lives to Christ while playing basketball. If we are serious about attracting 12 to 19 year olds to our churches, we need to take into consideration the influence of basketball, rap, and gangs on youth when developing outreach ministries.

Developing a basketball ministry does not require much. There should be 10 boys to 1 adult, access to a basketball court and basketballs, and men who understand the fundamentals. For many of our youth who play basketball, all they know how to do is run and gun. They don't know to pass, shoot free throws, play defense, and they're not in good shape. We need adult men who not only know Jesus, but also know how to play the game the way Magic Johnson and Michael Jordan played—four quarters of sound, fundamental basketball.

It would be great if these youth watched videos of the former center of the San Antonio Spurs, David Robinson, and the forward from the Los Angeles Lakers, A.C. Green. Brilliant basketball players who love Jesus and gave their lives to Him. They are principled men. Our boys need to see that you can excel in basketball and be strong in the Lord. We could create a new league and call it the David Robinson-A.C. Green Basketball League.

Every Christian leader, minister, and pastor reading this book should first ascertain the percentage of African American males between 12 and 19 that are in the congregation. Make a commitment to increase this percentage. Seriously study the impact that rappers, gangs, and basketball are having on our youth and provide workshops, seminars, and whatever you can do to bring attention to the mission of reclaiming our youth.

In the next chapter, we will look at another group that has been missing in action: young adult males 20 to 35 years of age.

CHAPTER 9:
YOUNG ADULT MALE MINISTRIES

When you think about the various age groups—children, adolescents, young adults, mature adults, elders—it's the 20 to 35 year olds who are in the prime of their lives. How tragic that the church has not been able to attract more men in this group and benefit from the strength, brilliance, excellence, talent, and energy of this highly significant group. Following the 12 to 19 year olds, young adults is the second least represented group in the church.

One of the most original ministries I have ever experienced is Soul Factory, pastored by Deron Cloud. I had the privilege of preaching for him. I encourage all readers to visit Soul Factory, which operates from three locations in the greater Washington, DC, area.

Pastor Cloud believes that in order to reach young adults, we must think out of the box. "This is the way we've always done it" no longer cuts it. Many pastors evaluate their ministries at the end of the year and if ministries are no longer effective, they are discontinued. My wife always says that if you haven't worn it in a year, you need to seriously consider giving it away.

Pastor Cloud uses seven principles to operate his church:

1. A clear evangelistic philosophy. They believe that church services and sermons are not the best way to attract new members. In this ministry, specific emphasis is placed on evangelism.

2. Financial commitment to evangelism. Soul Factory designates 60 percent of the budget toward evangelistic efforts.

3. Constant improvement of outreach.

4. A clear discipleship strategy. Pastor Cloud believes that the bi-weekly cell group meetings are fundamental to church growth.

5. Concert outreach. There are "All That Jazz" monthly concerts and "Go-Go Music Nights" that attract youth. In addition, a drama ministry is often used to deliver the sermon. This creative approach is used to teach the Word of God.

6. Targeted youth discipleship. This program is called Young S.O.L.D.I.E.R.S. It is an acronym for Sold Out, Living, Delivered, and In Everlasting Righteous Service.

7. Small group outreach events.

For churches that are committed to becoming more effective and relevant, Pastor Cloud recommends the following:

1. Spend your money on people, not real estate. This reminds me of Pastor Kevin Cosby in Louisville, Kentucky, who decided to build the Family Life Center before the sanctuary was built because he knew he could use the Family Life Center seven days a week. Until the sanctuary was built, the worship service was held in the Family Life Center.

2. Think outside the box. Try to be relevant. Don't evaluate your success by typical church standards.

3. Go with your gut. Don't try to duplicate the church experience. That will come in time.

4. Have a close support network, people who will tell you the truth and people with whom you can dream.

Earlier I suggested that a questionnaire be given to men or adolescents to ascertain their needs. The same applies to young adults. Pastors, Christian leaders, and elders don't always know the needs of the 20- to 35-year-old group. By listening to them I have learned that their greatest needs are:

- Money/job/economics
- Expunge felonies
- Fatherhood rights
- Sexuality/AIDS/STDs

As you survey 20 to 35 year olds in your church and community, I am sure the above needs will be revealed.

Remember, men want to be great. The church must become a place where this group can develop their greatness. If African American males between 20 and 35 do not feel that the church will give them an opportunity to be great, they will look elsewhere. The church cannot reach its full potential without men in their prime. It reminds me of a sports team that is attempting to win a game with its second or third string line-up. In order for the church to win, it needs to have its first string in the game. The first string is this age group, 20- to 35-year-old African American men.

Money/Job/Economics

Let's look at their first concern: money/job/economics. I've said it before and I'll say it again, if you live in a capitalistic, patriarchal country, survival is difficult with no income.

The following is a highly disturbing historical snapshot of Black fatherhood:

In 1920, 90 percent of youth had their fathers in the home.

In 1960, 80 percent of youth had their fathers in the home.

In 2006, 32 percent of youth have their fathers in the home.

Does slavery explain this phenomenon? Many peo-ple believe that slavery destroyed the Black family. Let's think about this. Slavery ended in 1865. As late as 1920, 55 years after slavery concluded, 90 percent of Black youth had their fathers in the home. Slavery did not destroy the Black family.

In 1960, 80 percent of Black youth had their fathers in the home. Some would say the Great Migration from the South to the North and industrialism destroyed the Black family. Yet 80 percent of Black youth still had their fathers in the home.

But in 2006, only 32 percent of Black youth have their fathers in the home.

The major reason for this decline is that the American economy moved from agriculture to manufacturing to information. The economy has changed, but our school system, its curriculum and pedagogy, for African American youth has not changed. Many schools are still preparing African American youth to work in manufacturing. What is a Black male to do when he has been miseducated, incorrectly placed in special education, has a high school diploma, and lower than a sixth grade reading level? How is he to compete in the information age?

Ideally, this problem needs to be corrected first in our school system, but as we saw in the One Church, One School program, if the school is not doing its job, then the church needs to step in.

Young males 20 to 35 need churches to develop economic ministries that will address their needs. I'd like to look at three churches that have done a tremendous job in the area of economic development.

My own church, Living Word Christian Center in Forest Park, Illinois, is pastored by Bill Winston. The church anchors a mall that we own. Our mall has numerous stores that provide employment for our members and the larger community.

In addition, we have the Joseph School of Business. It is a nine-month Christian business school that is accredited with the state of Illinois. It has a curriculum and certified staff that teach economic principles from a Christian perspective. The Joseph School takes its name from the same Old Testament Joseph who had the sense and integrity to flee from Potiphar's wife, and he also knew how to manage economic resources and prepare Egypt to withstand seven years of famine.

Upon graduation, Joseph School students are eligible to join an incubator. This provides new entrepreneurs office space, access to fax machines, telephones, computers, and copiers at greatly reduced prices. They have access to their professors (their mentors), to help them through the various challenges of starting up a new business. Eighty percent of businesses fail within the first five years. The Joseph School of Business is improving the odds for their students. This is an excellent ministry that I recommend all churches consider.

The New Birth Entrepreneur School is a similar ministry. Under the leadership of Bishop Eddie Long of New Birth Baptist Church, the school teaches emerging leaders how to start and maintain Christ-centered businesses.

Another ministry I'd like to lift up is led by Pastor Jonathan Weaver at Mt. Nebo A.M.E. Church in Maryland. In 1993, several pastors came together to create the Collective Banking Group. There are 85,000 churches in Black America with $50 billion in assets and $3 billion in annual revenues. Divide $3 billion by 52 weeks, and every Monday morning you have churches depositing $57 million in primarily White banks. These White banks make it extraordinarily difficult for church members to secure loans.

The Collective Banking Group has collected $100 million in deposits from various churches in the DC-Maryland area and has leveraged this with banks to create $250 million in loans.

My church, Living Word Christian Center, has gone a step further with the creation of New Covenant Bank. Numerous other churches, including Abyssinia in New York City, Faithful Central in Los Angeles, Crenshaw Center in Los Angeles, Trinity United Church of Christ in Chicago, Salem Baptist Church in Chicago, Allen A.M.E. Church in New York, and others have created economic development corporations. They use their growing economic power to acquire real estate in the community as well as provide jobs and entrepreneurial seed money for adolescents and young adults.

You don't get wealthy in America by working a job. In fact, unless you are the CEO of a major corporation, working 9 to 5 for someone else virtually guarantees a low-income or middle-income life, at least for the majority of African Americans. Wealth is acquired in three ways: entrepreneurship, the stock market, and real estate.

Entrepreneurship. Churches must teach young adults, specifically African American males between 20 and 35, entrepreneurship. While other ethnic groups are teaching their children that the way to get a good business is by getting a good education, African Americans are still telling their children that the way to get a good job is by getting a good education. We need to change that paradigm.

I strongly recommend that every church contact the National Foundation for Teaching Entrepreneurship. I have the privilege of serving as a consultant and board member for this organization. They are doing a fantastic job of developing materials and providing instructions for teaching entrepreneurship. From now on, our Bible studies should teach young Black males the Word of God and how to develop a business plan.

Ujamaa Model. Asians, Arabs, and other immigrants do not receive low-interest loans from the government to start their businesses in Black communities. They pool their resources with family members and others from their own community. Historically, culturally, and economically, they realize the importance of unity and Ujamaa in launching their businesses. African Americans should be doing the same.

Ujamaa meetings require the following:

1. Everyone comes to the meeting with a business plan.
2. Everyone brings $100 to the meeting.
3. Participants agree that the writer of the best plan will receive all the money.
4. The writer of the best plan agrees that he will support the other businesses present.
5. Members return the following week or month and repeat the process so that everyone who desires start-up capital will have the necessary funds.

Young Adult Male Ministries

Can you imagine if your church provided Ujamaa? If word got out in the community that ABC Church's Ujamaa program provides capital to launch new businesses, there would be standing room only. We say we want to attract Black men to our churches, but are we willing to listen when they say that economics is a major concern? Consider implementing a Ujamaa program at your church.

Stock Market. Every church should develop an Investment Club. These clubs will help transform young adult Black males from being one of the highest spending consumer groups in the country to savers and investors. The following guidelines are offered to help your Investment Club run smoothly and profitably:

1. The church will provide the club with initial seed money, let's say $100.

2. The pastor will choose a leader who has had success in the stock market and/or running investment clubs.

3. Men will learn how to read the stock pages. Over a year's time, they will learn the value of buying Nike stock vs. Nike shoes and McDonald's stock vs. a McDonald's Happy Meal.

4. Men will learn Rule 72: 72 divided by the rate of return will determine the number of years it will take for your money to double.

5. Men will pool their money and begin to buy stock.

Can you imagine if word got out that your church had an Investment Club, and African American males between 20 and 35 years of age were learning about the stock market and building wealth as a group? What an excellent way to teach the Gospel! The first hour would be devoted to Investment Club business, and the second hour would be Bible study. Both economic and spiritual needs are taken care of in this ministry. Once we have fed men economically, they will want to learn about the Word of God. They will see that it is because of the

Word of God that the church is in a position to run the Investment Club.

Real Estate Club. Young men must learn to appreciate the value of real estate. Real estate appreciates; when you drive a car off the dealer's lot, it depreciates in value—no matter how expensive the sound system or spinners. Young men need to be taught that the car note should never exceed the rent or mortgage. The following components make up our Real Estate Club:

1. Identify properties in foreclosure.
2. The church will provide the capital to secure one or more buildings.
3. Repair and rehab the property.
4. Sell the property.
5. Divide the proceeds and/or reinvest in another property.
6. Repeat the process.

Can you imagine if word got out that your church had a Real Estate Club that was purchasing properties in foreclosure, and that men were rehabbing these properties, selling them, profiting, and reinvesting the proceeds? As with the Investment Club, meetings are divided into business and Bible study.

Kazi is the Swahili word for work. Wealth is far more than dollars. It's human capital. What disappoints me about young African American males is that too many of them have been reduced to hanging on street corners in the prime of their lives. They are strong, intelligent, and talented, but because there are no jobs available, they have taken the position that without a job, they will do nothing.

To circumvent this state of affairs, I recommend Kazi. The program operates as follows:

1. The unemployed worker signs up with Kazi to barter his labor.

2. The church administrator sends the Kazi worker to work a certain number of hours for a client.

3. The worker's account is credited with the hours worked.

4. The worker then contacts the Kazi coordinator to receive those hours in the form of services from another worker.

The essence of the Kazi program is bartering and exchanging labor without the dollar bill as the medium of exchange. Can you imagine a church, like Soul Factory, where 20 or 30 brothers are bartering their labor? They cut hair, mow lawns, and other activities. When the dollar bill is eliminated from the process, we don't have to go without services because we can't afford them. Labor for labor, hour for hour, the process is honest and clean. I cut your hair, you mow my grass. We cannot allow the dollar bill or the lack of it to reduce Black men in their prime to accept their unemployed status. This is also an excellent way to gain on-the-job experience and may even lead to paying contracts.

Career Development. A much needed ministry is to provide job training, job placement, and overall career development (e.g., resume preparation, interviewing skills, etc.). The following strategies comprise the career development program:

1. Everyone is required to list a different career for each letter of the alphabet. So many young people feel the only occupations are NBA basketball player, rapper, or drug dealer.

2. Everyone needs to know that a high school dropout earns $6 per hour. A high school graduate earns $8 per hour. A college graduate earns $20+ per hour.

3. The blue collar hourly wage for painters is $15; highway construction, $18; crane operators, $20; truck drivers, $21; carpenters, $22; drywallers, $24; carpet installers, $24; plumbers, $30; electricians, $31.

Strategies to Avoid Being Unemployed
1. Earn a good education.
2. Become computer literate.
3. Communicate well.
4. Learn a blue collar skill.
5. Sell legal products that you like. You will never be unemployed if you know how to sell. Our young men can sell crack cocaine for 10, 12, 14, 18 hours per day. Surely they can sell Cisco, Lucent, Microsoft, Amway, and other products that the church can secure legally at wholesale prices. African American males would then sell at retail prices and reap the profit.
6. Be willing to volunteer to learn a skill.

Can you imagine how an unemployed African American male between 20 and 35 feels when he sees numerous highway and building construction sites in his community, but the laborers are of other races and ethnic groups? That is insulting and unacceptable. The church must organize its members and the community at large to express our frustration to local politicians. And if they refuse to address the problem, then we will simply create a disturbance at the construction site. Cars will not be able to go in any direction until African American men are hired. We need to put men in their prime back to work.

Expunge Felonies
Annually, 300,000 inmates are released from prison. Every one of our 85,000 churches must strengthen its resolve to help these men in crisis. These men are in the prime of their lives, and once they have done their time, they deserve a chance to live a productive life.

The One Church, One Inmate program was founded by Father Clements. With our 85,000 churches, that means four inmates per church. Or, from a larger perspective, if we have

1.5 million African American males involved with the penal system, then 16 inmates for every church.

Much more will be said about One Church, One Inmate, but I bring it up here because expunging their felonies is a major concern for young African American males between 20 and 35. The universal concern of men who fall into this category is that they have been released from prison, but because their past mistakes are still on the record, they are denied the opportunity to work. In some states, they are denied the opportunity to vote because of their felony status. Jesus taught us how important it is to forgive. Unfortunately, our government doesn't agree. We need to apply pressure on our representatives to pass legislation that will allow records to be expunged.

Fatherhood Rights

Many men agonize at how their ex is treating them as it relates to their child. I could give you horror stories of men who were current on their payments, but were viewed as economic mules and were not allowed to see their child. They may have arranged to see their child on a weekend, a holiday, part of the summer—only to have that denied because the ex wanted to show her vengeance. Unfortunately, many men do not have the economic resources to hire a lawyer every time the ex pulls one of her shenanigans. Men are resentful that the government seems to be more concerned about their payment status than about the mother providing time for the father to spend with his children.

I recommend the following strategies:

1. Pray and get someone to agree that you will get to see your child whenever you want.

2. Improve the relationship that you have with your child's mother.

3. Improve your relationship with your child's maternal grandmother.

4. Go on the offensive. Too many fathers react to the mother, the courts, and her attorneys. You need to become offensive-minded. You need to file suit to seek either custody of your child or joint custody, with you receiving the majority of the time with your child.

5. The church should provide free legal assistance to fathers in need.

Can you imagine if word got out that your church was providing free legal assistance to fathers in need of help? Many African American males are unable to pay the $500 to $5000 it costs to retain a lawyer. In this much needed ministry, churches would provide free legal counseling, filing of papers, court representation, and then, of course, Bible study.

Sexuality/AIDS/STDs
STDs have become an epidemic in the Black community. If a man is HIV positive in America, 45 percent of the time it's an African American male. Yet, African Americans are only 12 percent of the population. Most of the 300,000 African Americans who are released from jail annually have not been tested for HIV. The church must take its head out of the sand and address this problem, first by providing testing, medical treatment, and counseling. We will address this life and death issue in more detail later in the book.

Monday Night Football
What is the one thing that men of all ages, races, religions, and regions do on Monday night? They watch Monday night football! If you can't get the brother out of the house because of Monday night football, then bring Monday night football to the church! The opportunity to bond with other men while watching football will draw him out. As Pastor Cloud said, we need to think outside the box. Can you imagine if word got out that your church was sponsoring Monday night football?

Young Adult Male Ministries

With some physical development in the workout room and, of course, Bible study, you will have a full house.

For this **Samson** ministry, you will need:

- Food
- Television set(s)
- Exercise space and equipment
- Bibles

Pre-Marital Counseling

While pre-marital counseling is not often raised by young men as an issue, it should still be addressed. The divorce rate, 66 percent in Black America, is too high. It is unacceptable. The divorce rate is not much better in the White or Christian communities. Blended families and shacking up has become rampant in the church. Fornication and adultery are at an all-time high. Pornography is wiping out families.

I naively believe that Christians should have a lower divorce rate. The church should be a place where you learn how to become a better husband and father. Pre-marital counseling should help engaged couples think through the major issues that will arise in marriage, as well as determine if they are ready to make such a tremendous commitment. I have reviewed many pre-marital counseling programs in churches throughout the country, and there appear to be few standards governing these classes.

Does your church offer pre-marital counseling?

What is the divorce rate in your church?

How many classes are taught in your pre-marital counseling?

Are the classes co-ed, single gender, or both?

Who is teaching the class? Some churches have actually allowed single females, who have never married, to teach pre-marital classes to men.

When does the couple secure their date? If a couple is allowed to secure a date before satisfactorily completing

the program, they will not take the classes seriously. The wedding date should not be secured until the couple satisfactorily completes the classes.

What is your passing grade in pre-marital counseling classes? If everyone passes the class, what does that say about your curriculum?

Every man considering marriage should take a class in Ephesians 5:22–29. It is interesting that many brothers who do not go to church are well acquainted with Ephesians 5:22: "Wives, submit to your own husbands, as to the Lord." But men must learn all of Ephesians. Because it is so important to the survival of our families, community, and society at large, I present it here in its entirety:

"Wives, submit to your own husbands, as to the Lord. For the husband is head of the wife, as also Christ is head of the church; and He is the Savior of the body. Therefore, just as the church is subject to Christ, so let the wives be to their own husbands in everything.

"Husbands, love your wives, just as Christ also loved the church and gave Himself for her, that He might sanctify and cleanse her with the washing of water by the Word, that He might present her to Himself a glorious church, not having spot or wrinkle or any such thing, but that she should be holy and without blemish. So husbands ought to love their own wives as their own bodies; he who loves his wife loves himself. For no one ever hated his own flesh, but nourishes and cherishes it, just as the Lord does the church."

Scripture should never be taken out of context. It would behoove all men to read and ponder verse 25: "Husbands, love your wives, just as Christ also loved the church and gave Himself for her." If a man cannot love his wife the way Christ loved the church, i.e., *He gave His life for her*, then he should think long and hard about getting married. This is exactly the kind of self-knowledge that should be revealed during pre-marital counseling.

Even the most die-hard feminists are in line with God's beautiful marital order described in Ephesians 5:22–29. I have yet to meet a woman who resists submitting to her man—if she respects him, if she knows that he prays first and seeks her counsel second before making decisions. Ephesians 5:21 says, "…submitting to one another in the fear of God." The problem is that there are men who want their wives to submit to them, but they will not submit to God.

Serving the family as head of the house is a tremendous responsibility. My wife tells me all the time, "I'm glad I don't have your position." As the head of the house, you are the priest of your wife and children. You are to love your wife as Christ loves the church.

Verse 28 reads, "So husbands ought to love their own wives as their own bodies; he who loves his wife loves himself." You know how much brothers love their bodies. If you want to know where brothers are Sunday morning at 11:00 am, go to the health club, the basketball court, the golf course, the tennis court, the softball diamond, and the bowling alley. That's where you'll find men in their prime. Brothers love their bodies, and Jesus knew that. Therefore, Jesus made it real clear: "Love her as much as you love your own body."

That's why some of the classes in pre-marital counseling should be single-gendered. There's a need for men to learn the Word of God separate from their potential wives.

A Christian talk show compared this process of getting to know one another and self in the pre-marriage context to an employer interviewing a prospective employee. A woman could ask her potential husband the following questions:

What makes you qualified to be my husband?

Have you ever been married before?

Who taught you how to be a husband?

What are the qualifications for being a husband?

Do you love God more than you love me?

These are only a few of the questions women should ask their potential husbands. If the right questions are asked, the honest answers will determine if the man is truly ready to get married. We could avoid a lot of heartache, headaches, financial aches, and backaches in the Black community if only we, men and women, would ask the right questions before getting married.

A note to sisters: You may not like the answers your potential husband provides. Do not try and change a brother. As hard as it may be, accept that he may not be ready to get married, now or ever. This is a kindness and God's grace. You should know the truth before getting married, buying a house, and having children. The definition of misery is getting married to someone who never wanted to be married in the first place. The best brother will try to treat you well, but he will not be able to give you what you need if his heart is not in it. Other brothers will stray or indulge in pornography. So much pain could be avoided if only women would listen and accept a man as he is and not try to change him.

I once counseled a young 15-year-old male on some academic challenges. I asked him if he was sexually involved. He said yes. I asked him what would happen if she became pregnant. All he could do was shrug his shoulders. The major problem in Black America is not racism, unemployment—it's fatherlessness. What contributes to fatherlessness is Black men who have not been taught or do not accept Ephesians 5:21–29. To eradicate fatherlessness in our community, every church, pastor, and church leader absolutely must teach Ephesians 5:21–29 thoroughly to African American men in their prime.

In the next chapter we will look at the four primary culprits destroying African American males in their prime: prison, drugs, the street, and AIDS.

CHAPTER 10:
PRISON/DRUGS/STREET/
AIDS MINISTRIES

Let the following numbers jump out at you the way they jumped out at me:

- Total male prison population: 1,947,800. African American males: 842,500. White males: 695,800. Hispanic males: 362,800.
- 557,500 African American males on probation/parole.
- 200,000 African Americans have died of AIDS.
- Among men diagnosed with HIV, 45 percent are African American; 37 percent, White; 16 percent, Latino.
- 49 percent of Black men contracted HIV through sex with other men; 67 percent of them were unaware they were infected.
- 500 grams of cocaine, mandatory sentence. Five grams of crack, mandatory sentence.
- In 1980, 100,000 African American males involved in the penal system; in 2006, 1.5 million African American males incarcerated or involved in the penal system.

Is there a relationship among these statistics?
Is there a relationship among crack, prison, and AIDS?

Crack Cocaine

Slavery did not destroy the Black family. Even after slavery, with mothers, fathers, and children separated by different states, African Americans searched for each other. But there is now something that can separate mothers from their children, can make them do tricks in front of their children, and can make fathers risk incarceration and death. It is crack cocaine, and it is nothing to play with. Crack cocaine has had

119

a major role in destroying the Black family. This could be Satan's greatest trick.

If the church is going to be serious about saving itself, the community, and Black men, we must go after the greatest culprit, and that's crack cocaine.

I commend the Hip Hop summit for going after the draconian Rockefeller laws that have placed thousands of Black men in jail for excessive amounts of time for a nonviolent offense. Most African American males are in prison because of crack cocaine.

Churches must put pressure on their legislators to eradicate this 100:1 ratio between cocaine and crack. Why is it that the original drug (cocaine) receives a slap on the wrist and a homework assignment, and the derivative (crack) receives a mandatory sentence? Could it be because Whites are in possession of cocaine and African Americans are in possession of the cheaper drug, crack?

Did you know that 74 percent of all drug users are White, but 70 percent of those convicted for drug possession are Black and Latino?

In my rites of passage program, I always show a powerful clip in the movie *Godfather I.* The Godfather does not want to sell drugs, but the other four families tell him not to worry about it. "We'll sell it to the darkies. They're animals, and they deserve to die."

Drugs are an American problem, but regarding enforcement, drugs has become an African American holocaust.

We do not believe that there is a war on drugs. If that were true, drug enforcement would be going after the 74 percent who are using drugs. Instead, they go after miniscule, small time Black and Latino users. When there is a prostitution problem in affluent neighborhoods, law enforcement realizes that if they go after the seller, her replacement will be on the corner before the police can bat an eye. But if you're serious about eradicating prostitution, you don't go after Jane the Seller, you go after John the User.

The same is applicable to the war on drugs. If law enforcement were serious, they'd be going after the White user, not the small Black and Latino seller.

There is no war on drugs in America. There's a war on Black and Latino men. Churches must make this argument clear to their membership, the larger community, and local and national politicians. We need to demand an equal ratio of sentencing for cocaine and crack offenses.

The first ministry I want to lift up in this chapter is pastored by I.V. Hilliard in Houston, Texas, New Light Christian Center. Their Light Changers Institute is a free 90-day residential program for substance abusers. To make sure there is no conflict between church and state, the center is solely supported by the church. The program receives no government funding. For all those who are critical of prosperity preachers, you can't operate Light Changers Institute with chicken dinners. The members understand the importance of tithing. They have helped almost 8,000 men and women bind the demon of drug abuse.

This ministry knows that the best way to remove someone from the influence of drugs is to introduce him to Jesus Christ. Light Changers has an efficacy rate of 90 percent.

I can't think of a better ministry than Light Changers Institute because they've addressed one of the major problems in the Black community, and that's the impact of crack cocaine, specifically on African American men. Men in their prime who are addicted to drugs will tell you that their biggest problem is trying to find a residential facility that's available, affordable, and effective. Light Changers Institute is available, affordable, and effective.

Can you imagine if more churches had the vision of I.V. Hilliard to provide this kind of residential facility for men? Addicts do not struggle against flesh and blood but against principalities, powers, and rulers in high places (Ephesians 6:12). Eradicating this crack demon requires the blood of Jesus, prayer, the Word of God, and the Holy Ghost. Obviously, this would not be acceptable to a government-sponsored program, which is why Light Changers Institute is self-financed.

Free N One is another excellent ministry.

The Christ-Centered Approach To The "12 Steps"
For Addiction Recovery through
Christian Support Groups

1. Admitted we were powerless over addiction -- that our lives had become unmanageable.

2. Came to believe that, by accepting Jesus Christ as our Lord and Savior, we would be restored to sanity.

3. Made a decision to turn our will and our lives over to the care of God through His Son, Christ Jesus.

4. Made a searching and fearless moral inventory of ourselves.

5. Admitted to God, to ourselves, and to another human being the exact nature of our wrongs.

6. Were entirely ready to have God remove all these defects of character.

7. Humbly asked Him to remove our shortcomings.

8. Made a list of all persons we had harmed, and became willing to make amends to them all.

9. Made direct amends to such people wherever possible, except when to do so would injure them or others.

10. Continued to take personal inventory, and when we were wrong, promptly admitted it.

11. Sought through prayer and meditation to improve our conscious contact with God according to His Word, praying only for knowledge of His will for us and the power to carry that out.

12. Having had a spiritual awakening as the result of these Steps, we tried to carry this message to others, and to practice these principles in all our affairs.

Free N One is similar to the 12 steps of Alcoholics Anonymous, but it is biblically based. Every principle is connected to scripture. One of the strengths of this program is the opportunity to be part of a group. The Bible says, "For where two or three are gathered together in My name, I am there in the midst of them" (Matthew 18:20). There is power when men pray together, touch and agree, and publicly confess that they have a problem with a particular addiction.

While Free N One is not as strong as a residential program, it is still an excellent second choice. It can serve as a maintenance program following release from a residential facility, or it can be a stand-alone program. Churches should provide these ministries to not only their membership but to the larger community. Can you imagine if word got out that your church had a residential program or a biblically based Free N One ministry? If we are serious about attracting African American males in their prime to our churches, we must address this problem of drug addiction.

Salem Baptist Church, pastored by my good friend James Meeks, approached the problem from a different perspective. African Americans are only 12 percent of the population, but we consume 38 percent of all the liquor. Pastor Meeks, along with members of the Roseland community, were concerned about the large number of liquor stores and the sale of alcohol and drug paraphernalia in these stores.

Do you know how hard it is to get a Black community voted dry? It takes more than an act of Congress. It takes the Holy Spirit. That's exactly what happened in Roseland.

Satan did not go down without a fight, however. Government officials made it difficult with mountains of paperwork and bureaucratic red tape. Also, most of the liquor stores, owned by foreigners, were not going to give up their lucrative businesses easily. They brought in various liquor associations to help them maintain their occupancy.

Probably the most resistance came from the consumers themselves. Some African Americans literally told Pastor Meeks, "If you close my liquor store, I may have to close down your church."

Voter apathy was also a problem. Unfortunately, in many elections, only one-third of African Americans take advantage of the voting privilege. You can't vote a community dry if you do not vote.

Pastor Meeks and Salem Baptist Church went on the offense. They studied the issue. They met with the larger community to hear and understand their concerns. They then organized the community block by block, precinct by precinct. On any given day, 200 to 1,000 members would canvass the community to secure the votes. Change did not take place overnight. It was several years before Roseland was voted dry.

In the spirit of Jesus Christ, Salem Baptist Church even offered employment and opportunities to launch more useful types of businesses.

The moral of this story is that the community will not respect your church if a liquor store and a crack house are your neighbors.

Is your church in a dry community?

Are there liquor stores on your block?

Are there crack houses on your block?

Father Michael Pfleger of St. Sabina Church in Chicago, along with the community, decided that they would not allow any store to sell drug paraphernalia. They have literally shut stores down until they removed drug paraphernalia.

Do you have any stores in your community selling drug paraphernalia?

Study and adapt the great work of these ministries to the unique situation in your church and community. This is the least we can do in the name of Jesus.

Prison/Drugs/Street/AIDS Ministries

Incarceration

Since 1980, Black incarceration has moved from 100,000 to 1.5 million. This figure is simply unacceptable. In the spirit of Father Clement's One Church, One Inmate ministry, if we have 85,000 churches, and 300,000 inmates are released annually, all we're asking is for every church to adopt four inmates. If we have 1.5 million African American males involved in the penal system, all we're asking of African American churches is to adopt 16 inmates—One Church, One Inmate.

Do you have a prison ministry in your church?

How active is the ministry?

How frequently do they visit the prison?

What type of ministry do you provide?

Inmates have told me that the Nation of Islam, Jehovah Witnesses, and White male and female Christians visit prisons more than African Americans, and specifically, African American male Christians. Many brothers join Islam for protection because the rumor is, if you are a Christian, you're weak. But can you imagine if your church took the Ujamaa, Kazi, real estate, entrepreneur, and investment club ministries into the prisons how powerful this would be?

When you look at the demographics of inmates, there are several similarities:

- 90 percent of inmates enter prison illiterate.
- 80 percent of inmates are high school dropouts.
- 80 percent of inmates are fatherless.
- 70 percent of inmates were on the corners between 10:00 pm and 3:00 am when they were arrested.
- 70 percent of inmates did not attend church.

Does your church have a literacy program for inmates?

Do you provide free books and reading classes for inmates?

Most prisons have dropped the word rehabilitation. That is no longer their priority. America has a recidivism rate of 85 percent. The objective is not to balance the budget. They are aware that Head Start, Title I, Pell Grants, and job training are cost effective. They know that spending $28,000 per inmate per year with only a 15 percent efficacy is ineffective and inefficient.

Have you wondered why the inmates primarily come from large, urban areas, but the prisons are built in small, rural areas? Prisons have become big business, and maybe prisons are not designed to rehabilitate but to employ White males in rural areas who cannot find jobs elsewhere.

Churches must pressure their local politicians to build prisons closer to home so that ministering to and visiting inmates is easier.

I commend my church, Living Word Christian Center, for taking videotaped biblical foundation classes into prisons. Over the years, we have been able to bring hundreds of men to Jesus Christ as they are properly taught the Word of God. Salem Baptist Church has given every male inmate in Illinois a Bible on CD.

Expunge Felonies

Churches must help men expunge their felony records. African American males in their prime who have done their time cannot find work because the felony is still on their records. There are documented studies of wrongly convicted men who cannot secure employment because the felony remains on their record. Just as it would take virtually an act of Congress to vote a Black neighborhood dry, in many cases it would take the same influence to expunge the records of African Americans who committed a felony or who were wrongly convicted.

There is almost a 13:1 ratio of Black to White men who have had difficulties getting their records expunged. With no money, it is difficult to hire an attorney to help get records expunged. We need churches to provide free legal assistance to help African American males in this tedious process.

In my own state of Illinois, I commend State Representative Connie Howard and U.S. Congressman Danny

Davis. They have held numerous conferences and seminars that provide legal assistance. They were overwhelmed with the response of Black men who lined up early in the morning and stayed late at night, seeking assistance. Where is the church on this issue? Where's Adam? He's lined up around some other buildings trying to get his record expunged. If we want to be more attractive to African American men in their prime, we need to listen to their needs, and one of their major needs is to have their records expunged.

In addition, released men who have done their time need to have their voting rights restored. Forty-six states deny 1.5 million African American men the right to vote. Thirteen percent of African American men are disenfranchised. We're in a war in Iraq over democracy, yet we refuse to walk the walk and talk the talk at home. Ten states permanently bar inmates from voting, and that illustrious list includes Alabama, Florida, Iowa, Mississippi, New Mexico, Virginia, Wyoming, Delaware, Nevada, and Pennsylvania. If your church is in one of these states, you need to put pressure on your politicians to make sure that this is corrected.

Capital Punishment
Eighty percent of all executions in the United States occur in the South. The South is not only the stroke belt of Black America, it is also the execution belt. Stanley Tookie Williams did not have to die. He was doing good work in jail trying to increase peace and teach young people the benefits of nonviolence. There was much that we could have gained from his life and nothing to be gained in his death. Many research studies conclude that the death penalty does not deter crime and homicide. Unfortunately, Tookie Williams did not live in the 12 states that do not have the death penalty. Those states include North Dakota, Iowa, Hawaii, Massachusetts, Maine, Rhode Island, Vermont, Minnesota, Wisconsin, West Virginia, Alaska, and Michigan, along with the District of Columbia. If

your church is not in one of these states, you need to put pressure on your politicians to remove the death penalty.

The states that use the death penalty more than any other state are Texas and California.

AIDS

AIDS has now become the number one killer of African Americans. It exceeds homicide for African American males in their prime between the ages of 20 and 35. Forty-five percent of all men with AIDS in America are African American men. Of the men who have contracted AIDS, 49 percent contracted it with other men; 67 percent of them are not aware and are walking time bombs.

Three hundred thousand African American males are released from prison annually, and most of them are released without being tested. I commend Jesse Jackson Sr. and Operation PUSH for doing everything they can to demand that prisons provide the HIV test before a male is released.

Unfortunately, there have been tremendous challenges. The prisons do not feel testing is their responsibility. Some individuals do not want to know, and African American women have become the victims. Sixty-eight percent of all women who are HIV infected are African American women. African American women are only 12 percent of the U.S. female population. Black women deserve better. Black men deserve better. Where is the church on this issue? AIDS is the number one killer in Black America, yet some churches take the position, "They deserve to die."

What would Jesus do about this issue? I want to lift up two ministries that are doing great work in this area.

The Balm in Gilead

This ministry's first objective is to get past just talking about the issue because so many pastors are in denial. While AIDS has declined in the White and gay communities, it has increased, not only in the Black male community but in Black homosexual and heterosexual communities. You can't solve a problem if you're in denial. You can't solve a problem if you feel people deserve to be punished. People do not deserve to die.

The Balm in Gilead also teaches biblically based sex education. The church is like the parent who is so uncomfortable talking about sex with the child that he waits until the child is 18 years old to talk. The child smirks at the parent and says, "What do you want to know? I've been sexually active since I was 12."

Abstinence must be the core subject of sex education. We should teach the Word of God, that sex is only to be done between a man and a woman who are married—and married to each other. Even though we need to be honest, we have not taught abstinence like we should. Being quiet is not teaching abstinence.

More than 200,000 African Americans have died of AIDS. There are 56 million Americans who have an STD. Clearly, abstinence is not enough.

This is highly controversial, but The Balm in Gilead ministry distributes condoms. I understand the paradox of this issue. If we distribute condoms, it appears we're endorsing fornication, adultery, and homosexuality, and that we are not endorsing abstinence.

There is a population that's already sexually active, and they are infected. Many of them are unaware they are infected. Condom distribution will help save this lost generation. What better sanctuary to receive condoms than the church? I am aware that this is a sensitive issue. Pray and seek God's counsel.

Is your church in denial?

Is your church aware of the epidemic that AIDS has caused in the Black community?

Does your church provide sex education classes?

Faithful Central Church

I commend Faithful Central Church in California. They have created a ministry and an opportunity for dialogue called The Living Room. People come to talk about sexuality in The Living Room. There is no condemnation here. It is an opportunity for nonbelievers to come and kick it, discuss, share their pain, challenges, and trials.

The Living Room provides not only an opportunity for discussion, but also to secure HIV tests, STD testing, treatment, condoms, mammograms, and prostate cancer screening.

Does you church have a Living Room ministry? Two critical issues impacting Black America today are spirituality and sex. Sex and the church are always discussed in divergent terms, as if the two paths never cross. They do, often. The Living Room can become a place where spirituality and sexuality can be discussed together.

Street Ministries

There is a violent conflict between the church and the street. Can you imagine the church is having a homegoing service, and the gangs come in and literally take someone out and stab the person nine times? If the church does not take its message to the streets, the streets will take its message into the church.

Does your church have a street ministry?

Is your church in a gang infested community?

Does your church have any involvement with the gangs?

What advice and protection have you provided your young males who have to walk through these streets?

I want to lift up the ministries of Rev. Eugene Rivers in Azusa (Boston), Pastor Damien Lynch III, New Prospect Baptist Church (Cincinnati), and numerous other churches that have taken their ministries to the streets.

Azusa in Boston, Massachusetts, pastored by Reverend Eugene Rivers, has created the 10 Point Boston Miracle. More than a decade ago, Reverend Rivers was concerned about the large number of homicides in Boston. In the Black community alone, there were 62 youth homicides. As a result of Azusa, the Ella Baker House, Reverend Rivers, and others have reduced homicides 200 percent by patrolling the streets, mentoring young people, teaching them the Word of God, providing employment assistance and tutoring, and working in collaboration with the police department. The 10 Points are listed below:

- Establish four- or five-church cluster collaborations to sponsor "Adopt-A-Gang" programs that organize and evangelize youth gangs. Inner-city churches would serve as drop-in centers and provide sanctuary for troubled youth.

- Commission missionaries to serve as advocates and ombudsmen for Black and Latino juveniles in the courts. Such missionaries would work closely with probation officers, law enforcement officials, and youth street workers to assist at-risk youth and their families. They would also convene summit meetings among school superintendents, principals of public, middle, and high schools, and Black and Latino pastors to develop partnerships that focus on the youth most at-risk. We propose instituting pastoral work with the most violent and troubled young people and their families. In our judgment this is a rational alternative to ill-conceived proposals to substitute incarceration for education.

- Commission youth evangelists to do street-level one-on-one evangelism with youth involved in drug trafficking. Young evangelists would also work to prepare these youth for participation in the economic life of the nation. Such work might include preparation for college, the development of legal revenue-generating enterprises, and acquisition of trade skills and union membership.

- Establish accountable, community-based economic development projects that go beyond "market and state" visions of revenue generation. Such an economic development initiative would include microenterprise projects, worker cooperatives, and democratically run community development corporations.

- Establish links between suburban and downtown churches and frontline ministries to provide spiritual, human resource, and material support.

- Initiate and support neighborhood crime-watch programs within local church neighborhoods. If, for example, 200 churches each covered the four corners surrounding their sites, 800 blocks would be safer.

- Establish working relationships between local churches and community-based health centers to provide pastoral counseling for families during times of crisis. We also propose the initiation of drug abuse-prevention programs and abstinence-oriented educational programs focusing on the prevention of AIDS and sexually transmitted diseases.

- Convene a working summit meeting for Christian Black and Latino men and women in order to discuss the development of Christian brotherhoods and sisterhoods that would provide rational alternatives to violent gang life. Such groups would also be

charged with fostering family responsibility and
protecting houses of worship.

- Establish rape crisis drop-in centers and services for
battered women in churches. Counseling programs
must be established for abusive men, particularly
teenagers and young adults.

- Develop an aggressive Black and Latino curriculum, with
an additional focus on the struggles of women and
poor people. Such a curriculum could be taught in
churches as a means of helping our youth understand
that the God of history has been and remains active
in the lives of all people.

I never will forget when I attempted to implement the
work of Rev. Rivers in Chicago with our program, Community
of Men. When I called a meeting in our church, there were
about 150 men who responded. For two to three months, we
strategized on what we felt was the best way to address the
problem. When we were **inside** the comfortable confines of
our church, with coffee and doughnuts, 100 to 150 men would
attend the meetings. As long as we were only talking about
the problem, the men would participate. One of the many things
we planned to do was secure a building in the community where
we could direct the youth and provide rites of passage, Ujamaa,
tutoring, recreation, and a snack.

When it came to actually identifying a drug-infested
neighborhood in the community and going **outside** into the
street to pass out literature describing where the guns and drugs
were coming from, our numbers dropped down to 40 men.
Many community residents thought we were Muslims. I asked,
"Why do you think we're Muslims?" They said, "The Christians
do a lot of talking and praying, but they're afraid to walk the
streets."

That still resonates in my spirit. Is that true? When I talk
to Muslims and the Fruit of Islam about patrolling the streets,

they do not talk about fear. They talk about accountability and responsibility. There are consequences when men do not do what they were assigned to do. These delinquent brothers are visited by Fruit of Islam members. They hold those men accountable.

What happens in your church when men are absent and do not fulfill their responsibilities? I've asked God a million times, "Did you not see that Eve ate the fruit first? Why are you so hard on Adam?" God referred me to Genesis 2:16–17, where He reminded me that He did not give the instructions to Eve. He gave them to Adam.

I've asked God a million times, "Why didn't you allow Moses to enter into the Promised Land? All that mess he put up with dealing with those Negroes who wanted to go back to pharaoh." In Numbers 20, God tells Moses to speak to the rock, but Moses lost it and hit the rock. That infraction was enough to prevent Moses from entering into the Promised Land. God holds His leaders and men to a higher standard. We need men to be accountable. There must be consequences when men do not meet their responsibilities.

We need more churches to emulate the great work of Azusa and Rev. Eugene Rivers. We cannot allow gangs to control our neighborhoods. Jesus did not allow money changers in His sanctuary, and He would not allow gang members to control His turf.

In the next chapter, we will look at African American males 35 years and older.

CHAPTER 11:
MATURE ADULT MINISTRIES

Of all four age groups (infancy to 11, 12 to 19, 20 to 35, and over 35), mature adults (over 35) are most represented in church. And still, as with the other groups, there is a shortage of mature Black men in the church. If you compare the numbers of mature women 35 years and over to mature men 35 years and over, you will still see a shortage. Women outnumber men in every category we have discussed. However, of the four groups, mature men, especially over 50, have the greatest male representation in church.

As with the other groups, design a questionnaire to ascertain the needs of mature men in your church and community. Their major concerns include the following:
1. Mid-life crisis
2. Financial stability
3. Family issues
4. Retirement
5. Health

Men have a desire to be great and respected. Men want their lives to be significant. They want to make a contribution. They want their lives to mean something to society. Unfortunately, if men do not achieve this in their prime, between 20 and 35 years of age, there is a tendency to become melancholy and disoriented. They are not quite sure what they want to do with the rest of their lives. Some men experience depression, and that's another subject, like AIDS, that has not been properly discussed in the Black community or the church. Our collective denial has led to the increase of suicide rates in the African American community.

Mid-Life Crisis

As men age, testosterone production declines. This, along with other health changes, creates the mid-life crisis that leads to brothers buying red Corvettes, toupees, and other things to recapture their youth.

Some men express their disenchantment with an affair. An affair is an escape from reality. Older men want to know if they're still handsome. Are they still the sexual fantasy of women?

Look through the celebrity magazines and occasionally you will see a man in his 70s or 80s, on his deathbed, involved with some woman in her 20s or 30s (who is taking all his money). Remember the Pepsi commercial with Bob Dole watching Brittany Spears dance? This is typical of some men at this age.

Mature men are often disenchanted in their marriages, disappointed that their wives have gained a couple of dress sizes even though, if we're honest, men, we've gained a couple of pant sizes ourselves.

We've discussed the impact of pornography. Not all men have affairs, but too many have affairs with pornography. The wife no longer sexually stimulates them, and pornography becomes a convenient replacement. Given the high risk of adultery and pornography for men who are experiencing a sexual crisis, mature men must revisit Joseph to see how he handled temptation.

Remember Bob Dole's commercials for Viagra? Viagra and similar drugs have become a consideration for many men who are struggling with erectile dysfunction (impotence), perhaps for the first time in their lives. One of every three men, at some point in their lives, will experience some form of impotency, some more than others. This is a sensitive issue, but is there anything that we cannot discuss in the church? Whether we discuss it in church or not, whether we provide literature or not, believe me, it is on the minds of many men in the congregation.

In one of his monologues, Chris Rock joked about being the old guy at the club—but it's no joke. Have you ever seen a man who still wants to hang out with his children and grandchildren and go to the same parties and clubs they go to? This is a man who cannot let go of his youth or embrace his mature years. The church must step in to minister.

When a man begins to lose his hair, and when the little hair he has left turns gray, the mid-life crisis has begun. Your muscles are not as tight as they used to be. Your beer belly is showing larger than ever before. These are just some of the changes that occur during mid-life.

Does your mature men's ministry address these issues?

Another major concern is family. The life expectancy charts say that Black men precede Black women in death; still, there are large numbers of men who become widowers. You've heard the phrase, "You've come a long way, baby." Well, with women now in the workforce, they suffer the same stress-related, debilitating ailments that men do. They smoke, drink, do drugs, and have as much risky sex as men do. It is no longer an anomaly for a man to be the surviving spouse. Both my father and father-in-law survived their spouses.

How does a man cope emotionally and financially when his wife of many years dies before him?

What about those couples who stay together for convenience—for the sake of the children, because staying together was the right thing to do, because it was "cheaper to keep her"? This mature man is probably not happy in his marriage. His marriage may not have been made in heaven. He may not be the best of friends with his wife.

It's terrible to be in the later years of your life and you don't enjoy being with your mate. When your mate is not your best friend, when you've allowed the prime of your life to go by and she has grown in one direction and you have grown in another, it's difficult to reconnect. Friendship can help a couple endure through the challenges of mid-life. But what if you really don't like your spouse, much less love her? How does a man cope? Nothing is impossible with God, however. That's why ministering to the unique needs of mature men is so important.

I have learned over the years that one of the best ways to determine how compatible you are with your mate is to go on vacation together. At home, a couple lives in the same house, but they do not have to spend all their time together. When they're on vacation together, however, they are inseparable. They share one car, one room with minimal square footage, one bathroom, and a limited number of entertainments to choose from. If, by the end of the vacation, you can still laugh and joke with one another, you've got a good relationship.

Financial stability is a big concern in this age group. Most men define themselves as providers. During our prime, we set financial goals of how much we want to earn in a month or year. If we haven't met those goals during our prime, our mature years will be tremendously difficult, not only financially but psychologically. Greatness for men is tied to their financial prosperity. If they have not achieved their financial goals by mid-life, depression, fear, and despair can manifest.

Even with high Black male unemployment rates, responsible Black men will find legal ways to make money. Men tell me all the time that in order to make it in America, you need a full-time job and a hustle on the side. But what if a health crisis occurs and you are no longer physically able to work the long hours of your youth? This is no idle question, because in mid-life, the health chickens come home to roost. If you have not taken good care of your health, you will begin to suffer the ailments doctors say are inevitable in mid-life. They are inevitable only if you have failed to take care of yourself over the years and if you have been engaging in risky behaviors (drinking, smoking, doing drugs, and engaging in risky, unprotected sex). The good news is, however, that it is never too late to take good care of yourself, and a good mature men's ministry will pray with men and provide strategies to help men improve their health and vitality.

Important financial decisions are constantly being made during mid-life:

Do I buy food?

Do I pay for my astronomical gas bill?

Do I pay for my astronomical medical and drug bill?

It becomes even more complicated when men have to pay child support, especially to several different mothers.

Also on the minds and hearts of mature Black men are their relationships with their children. There is a tremendous difference between how Black America responds to Mother's Day and Father's Day. All the cards are sold out and all the restaurants are booked for Mother's Day, but there are plenty of cards and restaurants available on Father's Day. Unfortunately, many fathers will go to their graves never having reconciled the anguish and angst caused by strained relationships with their children.

Another major concern is retirement. Not only are there financial concerns, but there are lifestyle concerns as well. There is a proper way to retire. Unfortunately, many men have not mastered how to retire in style.

Men who have been providers all their lives don't know what to do with their lives during retirement. I have seen men retire from one job only to pick up another soon after, not because they needed the money, but because they didn't know what to do with themselves at home. They never developed any hobbies. They don't know how to relax. They only travel when it's related to work, never for relaxation. During their prime, these Black men were too busy working night and day to cultivate such interests.

Allow me to mention some of the creative things men can do in their retirement:

- Develop hobbies
- Walk
- Bowl
- Golf
- Tennis
- Swimming
- Health club
- Carpentry
- Drawing
- Painting
- Electronics
- Mentoring
- Tutoring
- Political involvement
- Spend time with grandchildren
- Help the homeless and the needy
- Visit retirement homes
- Get involved in various church ministries

The list of satisfying activities a retired man can do are endless. For many men, however, that's not quite what they were looking for because these activities don't pay the bills. Have you ever noticed that when women retire, they really retire to their homes. All the many things they wanted to do with family and friends are indulged in with pleasure. But mature men still need that hustle on the side.

I never will forget when I was speaking in Cincinnati and many men told me how fearful they were about retiring from the Ford plant. They noticed that when their colleagues had retired, within less than two years they had died. They had parked themselves on the sofa with the remote and a bag of potato chips, and in less than two years, they were gone.

These men were not ready to die, so they decided to stay at Ford Motor Company indefinitely. Even though they hated their jobs! How unfortunate that many men have reached that point where they are afraid to retire!

Wives tell me that there's a tremendous strain on the marriage once retirement kicks in. Before he retired, he was always at work, sometimes working two jobs, and she was at home. Now that he's at home, he wants to teach her how to cook, clean, sew, and do other things around the house.

Does your ministry help mature men prepare for retirement?

Health

I encourage you to read my bestseller, *Satan, I'm Taking Back My Health*. Listed below are some significant statistics:

- One of every two Americans will die of heart disease.
- One of every three will die of cancer.
- One of every six will die of diabetes.
- Black men lead the world in prostate cancer.

Is there a relationship between fried food, clogged arteries, and impotence?

Is there a relationship between eating three meals a day, seven days a week, but only eliminating three times? Where are the other 18 meals? Could that contribute to prostate cancer and colon cancer?

What is the relationship between African Americans consuming 38 percent of the liquor and high rates of liver cancer?

What is the relationship between African Americans consuming 39 percent of the cigarettes and high rates of lung cancer?

The following life expectancy statistics make the point clear:

- White women, 80 years of age
- White men, Black women, 75 years of age
- Black men, 69 years of age.

Let's review the above. Black men die six years before their wives and 11 years before White women. This is unacceptable. The research also shows that Black men live longer when they're married, and that insults my intelligence. They have to be married to live longer? It is true, when men are not married they drink more, smoke more, eat more fried food, and they don't take medical check-ups.

Large numbers of Black men have died of prostate cancer for no other reason than they chose not to be screened and tested. I commend churches that provide free annual prostate screenings to prevent this problem. Men do not need to die.

Some men will tell me, "I'd rather not know." This is foolishness. My wife reminds me that when people say, "It's my life. I eat what I want to eat," they need to remember that it's more than just their life. When you do not take care of yourself, other people have to take care of you.

It used to be that Black men died at 65 years of age, so there has been a four-year increase in life expectancy over the past several years. But don't let the medical industry fool you. The medical industry can keep you alive, but at what cost? I often ask my audiences, "Those over 40 years of age who are not on medication, please stand up." Few stand up. Our medical industry can keep you alive, but on a respirator, on expensive medicine, with arthritis in one leg and rheumatism in the other, with high blood pressure, or perhaps on dialysis three days a week.

The life expectancy chart measures quantity, not quality of life. John 10:10 reminds us that "Jesus came to give us life and to give us life more abundantly." Does being in pain and on medication sound like abundant life to you?

Does your church offer classes in nutrition? I don't mean a nutritional plan that recommends meat at every meal. As a vegetarian, I've been asked a million times where I get my protein. What I really want to ask is where they get theirs, because once you cook your meat, and you know Black folks like it well done, whatever protein was in your meat is no longer there or greatly reduced because of the way you cooked it. What I really want to say is, "Where do you think cows and gorillas get their protein from?" They get it from green grass, green food. Americans consume more protein than is necessary.

I often tease audiences that we'll all become vegetarians at some point. Some will do it voluntarily and some will do it grudgingly.

For some strange reason, it takes doctors a long time to recommend eliminating meat from your diet. After they have used every drug imaginable to address your health concerns, they finally tell you that you need to eat more fruits and vegetables, but unfortunately, it may be too late.

The mature years are when men realize that the clock is ticking and that life is short. For some elders, their social life is consumed with attending funerals each week. Their parties are now the repast.

Depression

As we become older, we lose those dear ones who used to provide us guidance and much wisdom. As much as we love our children, they don't provide the wisdom and conversation that our parents and grandparents provided. That's hard to accept, to live life without parents and grandparents, aunts and uncles and siblings. As a result, many in this age group become depressed.

It is only when you have a revelation of heaven, when you know that earth is not your home, and when you know that you will see your mate and loved ones again—that's when a man's joy is restored. Ministry can give him that.

Christian Maturity

The senior age group constantly receives bad reports. It is terrible for a man to go into the doctor's office and hear that he has six months to live or that he must stay on a drug for the rest of his life. It is a terrible time to be a babe in Christ. Now more than ever, the mature man needs to know his rights as a Christian. He needs to know he is a saint. He needs to know that death and life are in the power of the tongue. He needs to know that his Lord and Savior can heal him. He needs to learn how to pray with authority.

Many elders tell me they know the Bible, but I suspect they know religion. They've read the Bible from Genesis to Revelation like a novel. They know what's in it, but they don't have the revelation. One of the ways you can tell they don't have the revelation is the way they pray. When an elder says, "Maybe the reason why I have this cancer is because the Lord is trying to teach me something," that says something. Why would you pray to God to heal you if you thought it was God that put the sickness on you in the first place?

When an elder prays and concludes with "If it is Your will to heal me," you've just negated your prayer. Now you're in doubt—if if if! There should be no ifs! Every time Jesus saw someone sick, He healed them. Every time you pray, your prayer should be answered.

So here you are, in the doctor's office, a babe in Christ. The doctor gives you six months to live. If you are in a church or have prayer partners who do not know how to negate that evil report, your faith will be in crisis. Unfortunately, in this situation, a person may not even live the six months.

It is a terrible time to be in this age group and not know where the healing scriptures are. It is even worse to be in this age group and not believe the healing scriptures. It is catastrophic not to know your Healer.

In closing, I recommend that every reader in this age group do the following:

1. Drink eight glasses of water each day.
2. Take an adequate amount of vitamin supplements each day.
3. Eat three to five pieces of fruit every day.
4. Eat a salad every day.
5. Walk or exercise for at least 20 minutes daily.
6. Be open to enemas, colonics, vegetable juices, wheat grass, and acupuncture.
7. Read your Bible and pray daily, and you will enjoy the golden years of your life.

In the next chapter, we will look at the controversial issue of homosexuality. I wanted to avoid this issue, but the Holy Spirit would not let me. If we are going to develop strong men, we must honestly address this issue. We must be biblically correct, not politically correct.

CHAPTER 12:
A CHRISTIAN RESPONSE TO HOMOSEXUALITY

Just because someone is a homosexual does not mean that we cannot love him (her) or pray for him (her). Homosexuality is a sin, and like any other, it needs to be dealt with in the only way possible. It needs to be laid at the Cross, repented on, and never done again.

As a Christian, you should pray for the salvation of homosexuals the same as you would pray for any other person in sin. The homosexual is still made in the image of God even though he/she is in grave sin. Therefore, you should show him/her dignity as with anyone else you come in contact with. However, this does not mean that you are to approve the sin. Don't compromise your witness for a socially acceptable opinion that is void of godliness.

I often see in church bulletins and on church marquees that they are a Bible believing church. How Bible believing is the church that selectively takes out scriptures that do not reinforce what they want to believe?

I am not trying to be politically correct. I'm trying to be biblically correct. Let's see what the Bible says about homosexuality.

Leviticus 18:22: "You shall not lie with a male as with a woman. It is an abomination."

Leviticus 20:13: "If there is a man who lies with a male as those who lie with a woman, both of them have committed a detestable act. They shall surely be put to death. Their blood guiltness is upon them."

Many people will say, "Well, that's the Old Testament." I didn't know that we needed to separate the Bible and only accept one part and not the other. If that's the case, we need to have a Bible with just 39 books and another Bible that's just 27. We need to negate the Old Testament because Jesus was not in the Old Testament, even though if you read John 1 it clearly says "In the beginning was the Word, and the Word was with God, and the Word was God. The Word became flesh and dwelt among us."

If you must find it in the New Testament for you to believe the Word of God, listed below are two New Testament scriptures.

1 Corinthians 6:9–10: "Do you not know that the unrighteous will not inherit the kingdom of God? Do not be deceived. Neither fornicators, nor idolaters, nor adulterers, nor homosexuals, nor sodomites, nor thieves, nor covetous, nor drunkards, nor revilers, nor extortioners will inherit the kingdom of God."

Romans 1:26–28: "For this reason God gave them up to vile passions. For even their women exchanged the natural use for what is against nature. Likewise also the men, leaving the natural use of the woman, burned in their lust for one another, men with men committing what is shameful, and receiving in themselves the penalty of their error which was due. And even as they did not like to retain God in their knowledge, God gave them over to a debased mind, to do those things which are not fitting."

Nature vs. Nurture
The homosexual community is on a mission. If they can find research that documents that their desire for the same gender is because of nature, that they were born this way, then unlike adulterers, fornicators, thieves, and swindlers, they do not need to repent because this is the way God made them.

I have included this discussion in this book because of the impact that the homosexual community has had on men attending church. This sin hits men in at least two ways: the guilt that some men feel who are involved in homosexuality separates them from the love, forgiveness, and redemptive power of our Lord and Savior, Jesus Christ. Also, heterosexual men, seeing that the church is filled with women, children, and homosexuals, stay away in droves. So we have these two dynamics—self-condemnation and revulsion—working to keep more and more men in their prime away from church.

Some pastors and church leaders seem more concerned about being politically correct and not offending anyone than preaching the entire Word of God. They worry that if they preach the above scriptures, the exodus of homosexuals from the church will negatively impact their budgets. Some pastors worry that if they take a biblical position on homosexuality, they will lose key members—their music director, singers, and officers.

I have no interest in being politically correct. I'm not running for office, I'm not trying to balance the budget of a church. All I want to do is the will of God. I want to follow His Word. My major desire in writing this book is to increase the numbers of African American males primarily between the ages of 12 and 35 in the church.

Imagine a young street brother comes to church, but the few men present are effeminate—and the pastor is silent on the issue. I am in full support of The Balm in Gilead and the Living Room ministries. In no way do I condone the hostile nature that some churches have against homosexuals, i.e., that they deserve to die. Forty-nine percent of African American men who are HIV infected acquired the disease by having sex with another male. I want those men to live. My concern is what they are hearing or not hearing from the pulpit about homosexuality.

Pastors who rank sin and say that homosexuality is worse than all other sexual sins may be some of the biggest whores in the church. I want the pulpit to be just as clear as the Bible is on this issue. 1 Corinthians 6:9–10 says, "Neither fornicators, nor idolaters, nor adulterers, nor homosexuals, nor sodomites, nor thieves, nor covetous, nor drunkards, nor revilers, nor extortioners will inherit the kingdom of God." None of them! We should not be in the business of ranking sin. All activities mentioned in 1 Corinthians 6:9–10 are equally mentioned and none who indulge these sins will inherit the kingdom of God.

Sex is no longer for procreation but recreation. Some churches are so permissive that church members are living together (not married) and homosexuality runs rampant.

Allow me to digress a moment and extrapolate an analogy that I see in schools. If an African American male in high school is on the honor roll, AP classes, or in gifted and talented classes, he commits social suicide if he cannot fight, play basketball, and/or rap. The Black male peer group will not accept him if he cannot do one of those three things. As a result, many African American males do not apply themselves academically because of the tremendous pressures of the peer group.

Unfortunately, African American males who don't want to play basketball, fight, or rap, who want to do well academically, serve in the drama ministry, or express themselves through the arts are mercilessly teased and accused of being sissies and gay.

Homosexuality has increased in the Black community because of nurture. Circumstances, not biology, drive this sinful lifestyle. As a result, an extremely narrow definition of masculinity has been presented to young African American males. Young brothers who are interested in activities other than sports, fighting, or rap must do so in secret, and so the double life begins. It's a strong brother, confident in his masculinity, who can pull off being a chef, artist, actor, or any other nontraditional male activity. This is unhealthy and unnecessary.

When I was in college I experienced this. When I was on the track team I was considered macho. When I joined the debate team, I was considered gay and White acting. Thank

A Christian Response to Homosexuality

God my self-esteem was strong enough to withstand the pressure, and that gave me the courage to do what I wanted to do. Without my strong sense of self, I might have acquiesced and chosen the track team and negated my desire to debate. Had I done that, my career would have been greatly affected, and I might never have been a writer and public speaker.

There is a skewed definition of manhood, not only in America but in Black America as well. In my rites of passage program, I recommend that manhood be based on the pyramid, that we have an equal balance between being spiritually, mentally and physically strong. In the Black community, manhood is so skewed toward being physical that we are out of balance. I strongly believe in the principles of Maat: truth, justice, harmony, order, reciprocity, propriety, and *balance*.

How many men have we lost to homosexuality because they wanted to be on the honor roll, the choir, or drama department and bought into the lie that these were gay activities? How many men have we lost to these activities because they didn't want to be perceived as gay? How many men are hiding their true selves behind a macho façade because that is the only way to be a man in the Black community?

I want 50 Cent and Snoop back in the church. I want the people that like their music and follow them and their definition of manhood (a large percent of young men) in church.

Years ago, "research" declared that 10 percent of the American population is gay. This finding has been consistently shown to be based on a misinterpretation of deeply flawed research published by Kinsey. More recent, credible studies suggest that less than 3 percent and perhaps less than 2 percent of males are homosexually active in a given year.

Isn't it interesting how it is always the minority, the 1 or 2 percent, that has the loudest voice? For example, 1 to 3 percent of the U.S. has been trying to take God out of the Pledge of Allegiance, off the dollar bill, and prayer out of school. Now we're allowing 2 to 3 percent of the population to interpret and rewrite the Bible to say that homosexuality is not a sin. We should never allow a minority to dictate to the majority, especially when they are so against the Word of God.

Instead of the loud voice of a tiny minority, we should be much more concerned about our African American heterosexual brothers who have this warrior spirit and who are not interested in going to church because they are turned off by the homosexuality they see rampant there.

Let's now address the major issue that homosexuals are using to try and rationalize their behavior. If they were born this way, if it's nature, there's no need for them to confess their sin. That may be appropriate for fornicators and adulterers, but it's not okay for them because they were born this way. Let's dissect the literature on whether homosexuality is nature or nurture.

The premise that homosexuals use to rationalize their nature argument is the Levay study. Every single study that has emerged since the original Levay study falls into the above class: looking for or finding bi-modal, statistical, physiological, correlates to heterosexual vs. homosexual populations in both males and females. But however defined, results come with the same essential caveat: that cause and effect cannot be distinguished by the study.

There's a long tradition of investigating whether male and female homosexuals have abnormal levels of certain sex hormones as compared to their heterosexual peers. Speculation began in the 19th century that male homosexuals might lack normal male hormone levels and/or have female hormones, and female homosexuals the reverse. Several decades ago, reports of findings that seem to confirm such theories were not uncommon, though never well established.

The consensus today from research on males is that there is *no* substantial hormonal difference between homosexuals and heterosexuals. Research that was once thought to show hormonal differences in males has been shown to be plagued by problems in measuring hormones and inaccuracies in categorizing the sexual preferences of those being studied. The general consensus among researchers and theorists today is that hormone levels in adults do not determine whether a person is homosexual or heterosexual.

Mainstream media is reporting on the latest research that purports to show that gay males and heterosexual males respond differently to certain pheromones. "We cannot tell if the different pattern is cause or effect," says Dr. Savik. The study does not give any answer to these crucial questions. The same discussion arose after Levay's study, and he finally conceded years later that repetition of homosexual activity can change the brain to produce the effects he discovered. This study says nothing about homosexuality being innate, whether on a direct genetic or indirect basis. Likewise, if one changes the state of one's sexuality, the pheromone response will presumably change in consequence of behaviorally induced alterations in the underlying hypothalamic structures. Because it is tacit and not explicit, the widely held and erroneous presumption that brain structures are fixed and unresponsive to experience generates a second presumption also tacit. If a brain structure or function can be correlated to behavioral traits, then the trait must be both unchangeable and innate. Unaddressed and left nonexplicit, this two-step sequence of tacit presumption attached to explicit, high quality, scientific data, but only of a correlative kind, almost invariably generates in the mind of someone scientifically unsophisticated something akin to a belief.

Dr. Warren Throckmorton has also examined this latest study and draws the following conclusions:

"The study does not show involuntary hypothalamic response associated with self-assessed, sexual orientation. The study shows that gay males do react to the estrogen condition, but in a different manner than they react to the testosterone condition. The study cannot shed light on the complicated question of whether sexual orientation of the participant is hard wired. The brains of these participants may have acquired a sexual response to these chemicals as a result of past sexual experience. In other words, the response described in the study could well have been learned. The difference between identical twins and fraternal twins has been noted in many other areas of psychological continence. Identical twins very commonly develop a private language and communication that no one else in the family can translate. This can last for many years. Therefore, the twins study, identical and fraternal, does not establish any validity for organicity for homosexuality."[14]

I want to lift up a ministry that is doing great work in addressing the issue of homosexuality in the church, and that's Exodus International, the largest evangelical network of **former** homosexuals in the world. Note I use the word "former." For all those who believe that homosexuality is endowed by nature, how do we explain the thousands of men who have given up their homosexual lifestyle and have become heterosexuals and are now actively involved in the Exodus ministry?

The following is the mission statement of Exodus International:

"Through Jesus Christ, we found not only a way out of homosexuality and a path toward change, but ultimate healing and purpose in life. Exodus International is a resource and referral organization with over 130 member ministries across North America. It is the largest global network of **former** homosexuals and has been in existence for 30 years. Exodus International receives more than 400,000 inquiries each year from those affected by unwanted homosexuality. We have 105 local chapters, and what we do is put them in touch with a local ministry. Very often they'll have a weekly support group.

They immediately go into the support group and begin meeting other people. We recognize there's a certain danger in that. You have to have strong leadership and clear boundaries. Many ministries actually screen these individuals before they get into a group situation to make sure they really do know Christ and are really serious about change. So it's a building up situation rather than tearing down. It's local ministries that actually run these support groups."

Every church should implement an Exodus International ministry. According to the director of the ministry, Bob Davies:

"One thing that I challenge pastors to do is to give the whole counsel of God in relationship to the issue of homosexuality. We have done a terrific job of sending out the message that homosexuality is not God's intent for mankind. People know that in the gay community. They know somehow that the Bible says homosexuality is a sin. But often what I hear over and over again is that I never heard the second part of the message, which is, this is something that God can heal and forgive. I think that is the challenge that I want to issue to the church. We need to give that hope for a change. We need to remind people that it is a sin. Like any other sin, it can be forgiven by Christ. There are many people in churches today that are silently struggling with this issue. They don't know where to go. They have their radar out for a word of hope from people who have understanding and compassion. I think that if pastors would bring this up, perhaps in a message, in a newsletter, or at a Bible study, a neutral context and a message of hope, not condemnation and welcome hurting people who need help, they might be shocked at how many people in their church would come forward with hidden sins that they have never been able to bring out.

I'll give you one example. There's a pastor of a very large church in California who gave that message one Sunday morning. He said, 'If you're struggling with homosexuality, we want to help you and I want you to contact me this week. We will match you up with a man in the church who has never had this struggle. He will mentor you, walk beside you, and pray for you.' To make a long story short, within a month or two, they had a group of approximately 40 men who were involved in those kinds of relationships. That was the degree of struggle existing in that large church, and I think that is probably parallel in many other churches around the country. They just never had the invitation from the pulpit to be open about the struggle and to be invited to share with another brother in Christ."

As my pastor, Bill Winston, has often said in our church, "And if you really do believe that you were born that way, then in the name of Jesus, you can be born again."

EPILOGUE

I thank you for reading this book. I pray that you have learned from it, enjoyed it, and will buy additional copies to share with your friends. My major reason for writing this book is that we need to bring Adam Sr. and Adam Jr. back to church.

I'm even more concerned about the Adams who are between the ages of 12 and 35. If we don't reach Adam soon and reach him at this age, we will lose him to gangster rappers, gangs, the streets, crack, prison, homicide, and AIDS.

It has been my desire throughout this book to provide concrete ministries that address these issues on a daily basis. The church has become so theoretical and scholarly that we don't believe that we have the ability, models, and examples to do what God wants us to do.

A Sample of Strong Black Male Ministries

Hip Hop Haven / Holy Hip-Hop / Gospel Skate Nights

Monday Night Bible Study

Ujamaa / Joseph School (Economic Development)

10 Point Boston Miracle / Mighty Men of Valor (Security)

New Light Institute / Free N One (Drug Free)

Samson (Physical Development)

Rites of Passage

Shekinah (Youth Church)

Prison Ministry

One Church - One School

Exodus International / The Balm in Gilead / Sexuality (AIDS)

In closing, my challenge to you can be found in James 2:26: We need to be more than just hearers of the Word. We need to become doers of the Word. My prayer is that you will use this book and reach out to the community. If each of us can pull another Adam back to the Lord, specifically an Adam between the ages of 12 and 35, then we can make a difference.

To God be the Glory!

REFERENCES

1. Kunjufu, Jawanza. *State of Emergency: We Must Save African American Males.* (Chicago: African American Images, 2001) p. 157.

2. Bundschuh, Rick. *Passed thru Fire.* (Wheaton: Tyndale House, 2003) p. 61.

3. Murrow, David. *Why Men Hate Going to Church.* (Nashville: Thomas Nelson, 2005) p. 73.

4. Schultz, Thom and Joani. *Why Nobody Learns Much of Anything in Church.* (Loveland: Group Publishing, 1996) p. 136.

5. Murrow, op.cit. pp. 116-117.

6. ibid. p. 42.

7. Bundschuh, op.cit. pp. 47-49.

8. Murrow, op.cit. pp. 99-103.

9. ibid. pp. 140, 160.

10. ibid. pp. 64-65.

11. Sonderman, Steve. *How to Build a Life Changing Men's Ministries.* (Minneapolis: Bethany House, 1996) p. 39.

12. Smith, Efrem, and Jackson, Phil. *The Hip Hop Church.* (Downers Grove: Intervarsity, 2006) pp. 40, 41, 121, 201.

13. ibid. pp. 23-25.

14. National Association for Research & Therapy of Homosexuality. "Latest Gay Brain Study Scrutinized." Jones, Stanton, and Yarhouse, Mark. *Homosexuality: The Use of Scientific Research in the Church's Moral Debate.* (Downers Grove: Intervarsity, 2000) pp. 47-91.

Dr. Jawanza Kunjufu is available for
sermons
retreats
seminars
conferences
Bible study

Please contact 773-445-0322 (Telephone)
or
773-445-9844 (Fax)
or
ritask@africanamericanimages.com (E-mail)
or
African American Images
1909 W. 95th Street
Chicago, IL 60643

NOTES

NOTES

NOTES

NOTES

NOTES